TAKE BACK THE NATION

TAKE BACK THE NATION

MAUDE BARLOW
BRUCE CAMPBELL

KEY PORTER · BOOKS

Canadian Cataloguing in Publication Data

Barlow, Maude
    Take back the nation

Includes bibliographical references and index.
ISBN 1-55013-367-5 (bound)
ISBN 1-55013-398-5 (pbk.)

1. Canada – Politics and government – 1984-   .*
2. Nationalism – Canada. I. Campbell, Bruce,
1948-   .
II. Title.

FC630.B37 1991   971.064'7   C91-094824-0
F1034.2.B37 1991

Typesetting: Computer Composition of Canada, Inc.
Printed on acid-free paper
Printed and bound in Canada

Key Porter Books Limited
70 The Esplanade
Toronto, Ontario
M5E 1R2

91 92 93 94 95 96 6 5 4 3 2 1

CONTENTS

To the people of Canada, who deserve better.

ACKNOWLEDGMENTS

A book such as this reflects the work and insights of many people. We are ever grateful to the advisers and readers who helped us navigate over the tangled political and economic landscape of Canada. The book would not have been written without the solid support of Ken Wardroper, Tony Clarke, Judy Giroux, Errol Mendes, Ilse Turnsen, Bob Baldwin, and Duncan Cameron. Their patience and support are deeply appreciated.

As well, we are indebted to Susan Spratt and Marie-Lison Fougère for background analysis on the Constitution, Guy Daoust for his advice on French Canadians outside Quebec, Keith Kelly and Colleen Fuller for sharing their knowledge of culture, Mary Boyd and Jim Silver for their help on community organizing, and Steven Langdon for advice.

Lisa Shaw and Pierrette Landry gave graciously of their time to aid us in our quest for information, and Anne Boys of the Council of Canadians was unendingly patient with two harried authors. We thank them.

We also wish to thank Key Porter Books for trusting us in such an undertaking and for their unflagging support. Our editor, Charis Wahl, preserved our sanity. She is simply the best.

Finally, we wish to thank our families – Nathalie, Ryan, Andrew, Bill, and Charles – for their forbearance. Their love and backing of this project shine through its pages.

THE CANADA CLAUSE

The following is respectfully offered as a possible preamble to the Constitution of Canada. It embodies the essential characteristics that render Canada a distinct society, and recognizes the unique heritage of the three founding nations.

WHEREAS the spirit of the Nation was born in the ancestral homes of the First Nations of the land,
AND WHEREAS the people of Canada recognize as a fundamental characteristic of the Constitution, the unique, proud, and dignified nationhood of the first peoples of Canada, vesting in them the full protection of their existing and inherent treaty and aboriginal rights,
AND WHEREAS the spirit of the Nation was further formed from the pact of fraternity and co-operation that survived the battlefield between the first English- and French-speaking settlers of the land,
AND WHEREAS the people of Canada recognize as a fundamental characteristic of the Constitution, the linguistic duality of Canada that gives succour to the English- and French-speaking minorities across the land, and affirms the role of the Quebec and Canadian governments and legislatures to preserve and enhance the francophone society, culture, and language in Quebec and North America,
AND WHEREAS the spirit of the Nation has been nurtured in the environment of the evolving multi-cultural reality of the land,

AND WHEREAS the people of Canada recognize as a fundamental characteristic of the Constitution, the multicultural present and future of all regions of Canada,
AND WHEREAS the Canadian people have demonstrated their unique identity to the Community of Nations through their diversity of regions, cultures, and languages, creating a union that enshrines both respect for difference and for the fundamental individual and collective rights of humanity, including substantive equality for those discriminated against by reason of gender, racial origins, colour, religion, age, or disability,
THEREFORE, we the people of Canada declare the following to be the supreme law of the land:

Errol P. Mendes
Editor-in-chief, *National Journal of Constitutional Law*

INTRODUCTION

Canada faces extinction as an independent nation. It is threatened by the effects of the present government's destructive policies: crisis levels of unemployment and poverty, deep cuts to the economic base, sustained attacks on social programs and cultural institutions, weakening East-West ties, and the imminent withdrawal of Quebec from Confederation. It is threatened also by an alliance of corporate leaders and conservative politicians who aim to extend the Canada-U.S. Free Trade Agreement to Mexico and throughout the hemisphere.

It is time to consider what alternatives remain open to us as a nation, and their cost.

There exist in Canada three fundamental and historic tensions that rise to the surface from time to time to challenge our most revered beliefs and the harmony of our national systems:

- the lure of closer economic and political ties to the United States,
- regional rivalries, misunderstandings, and power struggles,
- the long-unresolved conflict between the French- and English-speaking peoples of Canada.

This is the first time in our history, however, that all three have surfaced at the same time, creating crises, setting deadlines, and demanding resolution. Continental trade deals threaten the very existence of our manufacturing sector; the economy seems unable to recover from the massive loss of jobs and companies. Regional alienation, resentment, and jealousy are building; provinces, reeling from the deep cuts to federal transfer payments, demand powers once considered sacred to the national cause. And Canada must offer an economic and political alternative that might — or might not — pre-empt a referendum on whether or not Quebec should remain a part of Canada.

In addition are the demands — now unstoppable at last — for full accountability to Canada's aboriginal peoples. Their urgent call for justice will necessitate major land-claim, constitutional, and self-government settlements.

Canadians are overwhelmed by the crisis looming before them and, for the most part, feel powerless to prevent what appears to be the destruction of their nation. Political institutions have allowed the imminent breakup of Canada. The financial instability of the country is mirrored in the dislocated lives of individual Canadians. We see our precious social systems dying and know that, in a few years, Medicare may be just a memory from a past when Canadians held different values.

Above all, Canadians know that the person who should be leading the rescue from this crisis is a vital part of the problem. Prime Minister Brian Mulroney has neither the public trust nor the moral authority to speak for Canadians. He has done more than any person in Canadian history to destroy this country. His economic policies are disastrous, and he played politics with the most delicate constitutional issues. Yet his government still has two years to do more damage. With no political way to remove him from office, Canadians are becoming increasingly disheartened.

This sense of defeat is dangerous. There is a great deal of anti-Mulroney feeling, but much of it is unfocused and without a clear alternative. As well, it is crucial to understand that he alone is not the problem. The pressure to maintain the corporate-friendly policies Brian Mulroney has followed would still be there without him.

Some Canadians are venting their frustration in anti-Quebec sentiment, which is pointless, wrong-headed, and ultimately self-defeating. Some have turned to "quick fix" political parties and movements that find easy scapegoats in immigrants, French-speaking people, and natives, and offer policies that would destroy the very foundations of Canada. Yet others are retreating into apathy and surrender. They feel powerless to avert the crisis and believe that the forces destroying Canada are beyond their control.

Take Back the Nation is a call to arms. Canadians can and must take charge of their lives and the future of their country. To do so, we must first analyse the problem. What is happening in Canada is not the accumulation of a number of unconnected accidents. It is the systematic destruction of a nation. It is the callous dismantling of a way of life that does not serve the interests of the large corporate powers of North America and the governments that back them. Abandoning a separate Canadian economy is an act of economic self-destruction. It has weakened the foundation of the Canadian state; together with the government's decentralization policies, it has hastened the political breakup of the country.

Canadians are fighting back. In small communities and large, they are seeking ways to take control of their lives, their economy, and their future. *Take Back the Nation* offers economic and political solutions to the crisis facing Canada. Canada and Quebec can live in harmony and mutual respect by challenging the common enemies of both: poverty, violence, racism, diminishing economic prospects, and the radical corporate agenda that is under-mining social advancement.

What we offer is a blueprint for survival and concrete actions all Canadians can take — as communities and as individuals. If the powers in government cannot save our nation, the Canadian people must.

And we shall.

PART ONE

CANADA IN CRISIS

1.

THE SUBVERSION OF THE NATIONAL ECONOMY

"The confrontation between the voices of the corporate elite and ourselves has revealed a fundamental conflict between competing moralities."

— Remi DeRoo,
Bishop of Victoria

THE CREATION OF CANADA WAS A DELIBER-
ate act by a community, the formation of a government to express and enforce its fundamental values. That act included evolving laws, regulations, and institutions to govern economic activity: how companies compete, how they treat their workers, how much taxes they pay, what environmental standards they must meet, what areas of enterprise are reserved solely for government, how wealth is created, and how it is divided.

In short, building a distinct Canadian economy was inseparable from building a nation. What happens when you tear down what is distinct in the economy and fuse what's left to another economy, especially to the largest in the world? Can the Canadian economy, can the nation itself express the values of the community? When does Canada cease to be Canada?

Peter Francis is one of the few Canadian businessmen

who publicly opposed free trade. A diminutive man with a thick Scottish accent and a smile you can wrap yourself in, he fought the Conservative initiative from the beginning. Francis was the president of ACF Grew Inc., a Canadian boat manufacturer based in Penetanguishene, Ontario. Grew had a reputation for quality and was described in the trade as "unquestionably the largest and most successful manufacturer of power boats in Canada."

Testifying before a parliamentary committee in 1985, Francis was not intimidated by taunts that opponents of free trade were weak and inefficient. He saw clearly the real dangers of fighting the U.S. giants, with their huge production, financial, marketing, and distributional advantages, in a continental market. "We are geared to a population of twenty-five million," he said. "The task of expanding to compete in a market of two hundred and fifty million is staggering." The Canadian power-boat industry was protected by a 15 percent tariff and a 71-cent dollar. How much more staggered would Francis have been had he foreseen an 86-cent dollar and interest rates five points higher than those of his U.S. competitors?

Francis took particular offence at the view of fellow witness, business professor John Crispo. "He [Crispo] sees 'some dislocation' to small industries. I see my business, in which I have invested time and money, disappearing. He sees 'some small dislocation' of workers. I see two hundred and fifty families known to me personally suddenly faced with the unemployment of a breadwinner with little hope of securing new employment because his skills are peculiar to our industry."

ACF Grew Inc. declared bankruptcy in the fall of 1988, an early casualty of the free-trade era. Its major Canadian rival, Doral Boats, remained afloat by recently opening a plant in Clinton, Tennessee. Since the free-trade deal went into effect, 25,000 Canadian companies have followed Grew into bankruptcy, the highest rate in Canadian history.

Living Under Economic Occupation

Canada is the most economically occupied country in the industrial world; no other country even comes close. More than half of our manufacturing sector is under foreign control. We have learned from years of experience that, left to their own devices, foreign corporations may act contrary to Canadian economic interests, destroying more jobs than they create, and killing off Canadian competitors. They import more, export less, and are less likely to use local suppliers than are Canadian firms. Three-quarters of U.S. exports to Canada are transfers from U.S. parents to their Canadian subsidiaries, rather than exchanges on the open market.

The purpose of foreign-investment regulations was to give government the leverage to ensure that transnational corporations made commitments that benefited the Canadian economy. It was also to reduce gradually the level of foreign ownership in Canada.

Free trade replaced the national market with a continental market and greatly hampered the ability of government to regulate corporations. Not only did they no longer have to be good corporate citizens while in Canada, they didn't even have to stay in order to sell into the Canadian market.

The withdrawal of the obligation on foreign companies to produce in Canada has dramatically changed U.S. subsidiaries here. Rather than becoming export platforms into the new continental market, branch manufacturing plants are simply shutting down. If they leave anything behind, it is just a warehouse or a sales office. The Canadian market can now be supplied merely by adding an extra shift or by filling unused capacity at a U.S. or Mexican plant. As Adam Zimmerman, vice-chairman of Noranda Inc., said, "If you can move a plant, why would you stay here?" Scores of companies have closed their Canadian purchasing or marketing divisions. Many have eliminated their Canadian boards of directors and absorbed their subsidiary so that it is no longer a separate legal entity.

The consequences of this transformation are evident in the enormous casualties in the manufacturing sector. Services closely linked to manufacturing, such as computing, engineering, advertising, and other business services, are also hurting.

Wayne McLeod is the president of CCL Industries Inc., which makes cans and a range of customized consumer products. Under free trade his main customers, the U.S. transnationals, either shut down entirely or closed their Canadian purchasing divisions. CCL has survived by becoming, in practice if not formally, an American company. Before free trade, two-thirds of its production was located in Canada. Today, more than two-thirds of its production facilities are south of the border. It recently closed a Toronto factory employing over two hundred.

The Canadian economy has been going through a profound crisis during the last three years, by many measures the worst since the Great Depression of the 1930s. We are witnessing a rapid deindustrialization. One manufacturing job in five has disappeared, and manufacturing employment has dropped from 17 to 15 percent of our workforce since 1988, the lowest such rate in the industrial world. During the 1982 recession, less than 25 percent of Ontario's manufacturing job loss was attributable to permanent plant closures. In the present crisis, 66 percent of the jobs lost are the result of permanent closures. Akio Morita, president of Sony Corp., warned a Canadian audience several years ago of the dangers of permanently hollowing out manufacturing: "In the long run a country that has lost its manufacturing base has lost its vital centre. A service-based economy has no engine to drive it."

The current economic crisis is no accident. It is the planned consequence of policies executed since 1984 by the Conservative government in alliance with big business, in order to change radically the Canadian economy. Brian Mulroney, his Tory cabinet, and the Business Council on National Issues (BCNI), the cabinet of big corporations led by Thomas d'Aquino, set out to transform the Canadian economy from a distinctly national to a regional one within an integrated continental economy dominated by the United States.

The corporate sector found in the government of Brian Mulroney the clearest and most committed expression of its interests of any Canadian government in history. Indeed, Brian Mulroney promised at the beginning of his mandate to remake a Canada that would be "unrecognizable."

The BCNI is the single most powerful economic and political body in the country. More than a third of its members are foreign, mainly U.S.-owned, and include some of the most powerful transnational corporations in the world. Whether they are Canadian or foreign, their first loyalty is to business and their own survival and growth within the global economy. Any loyalty to Canada or to a national market is, at best, secondary.

The Conservative/corporate tandem sought to transform the nation into Canada Inc. through massive deregulation and privatization in a merger with America Inc. in a free-trade deal. The market, with a "supportive" government climate, would do the rest, restructuring and harmonizing the economy along continental lines.

In the corporate vision of a "borderless" or "globalized" economy, Canada as a separate economic entity is obsolete. The Canadian economy is the product of specific government policies, often in defiance of market forces. Now, more than ever, these are a restraint on the corporations' ability to grow and prosper, to be internationally competitive. So, the transnationals argue, the power of the government has to be reduced to enable the corporations to roam freely.

As national economies everywhere have weakened and markets have transnationalized, corporations need no longer have a vested interest in ensuring that their citizens have sufficient incomes to buy what the corporations produce. No longer must they accept governments and unions as necessary vehicles for redistribution, for keeping upward pressure on incomes. If demand falls in Canada because of falling middle-class incomes, there is new demand elsewhere in the continental or global economy, which more than compensates. Indeed, there may be an advantage: lower incomes mean lower costs and therefore greater competitiveness.

The Corporate Agenda
The Conservative/corporate action plan to dismantle the country has been devious and convoluted in its implementation. However, the concept itself is really quite simple. For convenience we have broken it into seven strands that are intricately woven into a fabric. The strands reinforce one another, and the effect is greater than the sum of its parts.

Here is their action plan.

1. Tie the Canadian economy by a free-trade agreement to the most powerful economy in the world, in which the corporate sector controls the government's agenda and an

unfettered "free-market ideology" is firmly entrenched. This free-trade agreement is a constitution of corporate rights that reduces and circumscribes the power of governments, an international treaty that protects this new order from change or reversal by subsequent governments. Say the agreement will make Canada stronger. Say it will create jobs.

Use the integration of the two economies as a lever to reshape the Canadian economy in the U.S. image. Integration of the smaller into the larger leaves no choice, as the economies must mirror each other. Force "economic restructuring," i.e., cut jobs. Force "alignment of cost structures," i.e., force down wages, weaken union bargaining power, force down labour laws and environmental standards, force down taxes, force down government spending on social programs, etc. Do it in the name of harmonization. To harmonize means to Americanize.

2. Use monetary policy, that is, interest rates and exchange rates, to speed up restructuring. To weed out "weak" companies, accelerate the loss of jobs and the downward pressure on wages by speeding up import competition and creating a recession. Nothing will produce mass unemployment as fast as a high–interest-rate policy combined with a policy to cut public spending. High unemployment keeps wage demands low. Also, a high–interest-rate policy is a good way to transfer more wealth to those who have wealth.

In the name of fighting the deficit, use high interest rates to increase the deficit. Focus public attention on the "urgency" to reduce the deficit as a smokescreen to hide the slashing of public spending.

3. Bring in tax subsidies for high-income earners and large corporations. Say the purpose is to free up private savings and unleash the entrepreneurial energies of Cana-

dian business. Increase taxes for middle-income earners and the working poor. Where possible, do it surreptitiously through mechanisms such as the inflation de-indexing of tax brackets.

4. Cut back social programs, especially the universal ones. Do it in the name of targeting those who need them most. Delink programs from cost-of-living increases, so that they lose value automatically and gradually. Shift the burden of providing these programs to the provinces. Apologize, but say the deficit crisis leaves no choice. Get the provinces on side by giving them more power.

Weakening social protections and creating high unemployment produce a more fearful and more compliant work-force — willing to work at low-skill, low-pay jobs; willing to work at part-time or temporary jobs; and willing to move to where the jobs are. A "flexible," undemanding work-force increases competitiveness.

5. In the name of fighting inflation, strengthen measures such as sales taxes (GST) and high interest rates, which actually increase inflation. As inflation rises, weaken the bargaining power of workers to keep wages apace. Do this directly to public-sector employees by imposing a wage freeze.

6. Privatize profitable public-sector enterprises. Return them at attractive prices to the corporate sector or offer shares to high-income Canadians. Deregulate sectors of the economy. Privatization and deregulation, while bolstering corporate profits, usually result in higher prices to consumers or poorer-quality products, or both. They also kill jobs, depress wages, and weaken unions.

7. Bring in all these policies in the name of international competitiveness. Say competitiveness will bring more jobs and greater prosperity, but be vague about when. Also say that, to be competitive, Canadian workers

have to reduce wages and social protections. Argue that, in an increasingly competitive world, we have no choice, we must adjust. Place the burden of adjustment on ordinary Canadians who are disrupted and dislocated by this corporate-driven adjustment process.

Analysts disagree on the causes of the current economic crisis and the extent to which it can be blamed on free trade. However, there is one point on which all agree: the government's high–interest-rate policy has been a major cause. Moreover, this policy has been deliberate. In October 1990, Michael Wilson told the House: "We have had made-in-Canada growth. It developed into a made-in-Canada problem so we imposed a made-in-Canada solution. . . ." At the same time, Brian Mulroney told a Montreal audience: "We will not be diverted from our obligation to wring as much inflation as we can out of the economy, even if in the process we are induced into a slowdown." The policy has driven up the value of the Canadian dollar and paralysed economic activity. It has forced thousands of Canadian companies out of business or out of the country. It has forced thousands of people into personal bankruptcy and put hundreds of thousands of people out of work. It has caused, as former Alberta premier and free-trade advocate Peter Lougheed admits, "irrevocable damage" to the Canadian economy.

The finance minister and the Bank of Canada governor argue that it has been necessary to stamp out growing inflation, particularly from rising wage demands, as the unemployment rate had fallen below its "natural" rate of 8 percent.

Yet there was little evidence of a building inflationary spiral driven by wages. Wage settlements were consistently behind price increases, and had been since the early

1980s. Indeed, high interest rates were themselves pushing up prices. Business borrowers were passing on their higher borrowing costs to their customers; higher mortgage rates were boosting the cost of housing; and so forth.

The Conservatives also said that interest rates were being pushed up by government borrowing in order to finance its huge debt, and that the sooner the government could cut spending and reduce its debt the sooner interest rates would come down. There is no evidence to support this claim.

National financial markets have become highly integrated globally. Foreigners now hold 40 percent of the federal government debt. As the U.S. dollar is the main currency of international exchange, U.S. interest rates determine the cost of borrowing on international financial markets. Canadian interest rates can never be far out of line from U.S. interest rates. If the Bank of Canada sets its interest rate too low, money — both Canadian and foreign-owned — will flow out, the demand for Canadian dollars will drop, and the value of the dollar will fall relative to the U.S. dollar. If the Bank increases its interest rate relative to the U.S. rate, money will flow in, pushing up the value of the dollar relative to that of the U.S. dollar.

The Bank of Canada deliberately engineered just such a rise in interest rates in 1988. This move attracted American, German, Japanese, and other foreign investors to buy government debt and, in the process, to push up the value of the Canadian dollar. Increased interest payouts to foreign and Canadian creditors raised the deficit and, over time, the debt. Thus high interest rates have pushed up both the debt and deficit, not the other way around.

The goal of declaring inflation Public Enemy Number One was misguided, but, even so, high interest rates were a crude instrument for fighting it, and their cost to the economy was brutally high. The proof of that is before us now, and the inflation rate is still higher than it was before the high-interest, anti-inflation campaign began in earnest back in 1988.

Critics of the free-trade agreement believe that the Mulroney government made a secret commitment to the Americans to raise the value of the Canadian dollar relative to the U.S. dollar. Chief trade negotiator Simon Reisman dismisses the hypothesis with his usual tact and subtlety: "It is just a stupid allegation by a bunch of stupid people." However, as the government continues to hold to its destructive policy, even free-trade supporters have come to suspect that a deal on exchange rates may have been made.

Former Tory industry minister Sinclair Stevens fuelled this suspicion when he told *The Toronto Star* that his U.S. counterpart, commerce secretary Malcolm Baldridge, "drove it home to me" in late 1985, six months before the beginning of formal negotiations, that a dollar deal was the key to getting a free-trade agreement. Baldridge told Stevens that it would have to rise close to the 90-cent range. At the time the dollar was trading at 71 cents U.S.

Commerce secretary Baldridge, the main spokesperson for American corporate interests and then-treasury secretary James Baker were closely involved in the talks. American business saw the low Canadian dollar as an unfair subsidy to Canadian exporters. The U.S. National Association of Manufacturers warned that there could not be a free-trade agreement unless there was a deal on exchange rates. They saw the negotiations as a way to force up the Canadian dollar and thereby reduce Canada's trade surplus with the United States, which was $20 billion in 1985.

Chief U.S. trade negotiator Peter Murphy was also very interested in the exchange-rate issue. In a memo to his negotiating team in April 1986, just after the Senate Finance Committee had given him the green light to start formal talks, Murphy wrote that movement on the Canadian exchange rate was one of his six major negotiating priorities.

Eight months later, Murphy told an elite New York gathering of American and Canadian businesses that, although the exchange rate was not formally on the free-trade bargaining table, the U.S. Congress saw it and free trade as "inextricably linked" and would not, in his view, approve a trade deal without exchange-rate concessions. He added that Secretary Baker was handling the matter.

Indeed he was. Months earlier, Baker was reported as saying that Canada might have to raise the value of its dollar as the price of admission into the so-called Group of Five (G-5), the inner circle of industrial nations that met behind closed doors to co-ordinate their economic policies. The dollar was trading at 72 cents at the time.

The Ontario treasury ministry was following the issue very closely, worried about the consequences if the federal government caved in. Its own study showed that, for every 5-cent rise in the dollar, 140,000 jobs would be lost. It also concluded that the exchange-rate question would probably be handled at the G-5 forum.

Less than two weeks before the U.S. Congressional deadline of October 3, 1987, a shaken Simon Reisman went before the television cameras to say that the negotiations had broken down. Michael Wilson and James Baker, the financial czars, took over from the negotiators and struck a deal minutes before the deadline. The dollar had climbed gently to 75 cents.

A year later it had soared to 83 cents, and since the beginning of 1989 the dollar has stayed between 85 and 87 cents. Currency traders have observed that the Bank of

Canada intervenes very heavily in the currency markets when necessary to ensure that the dollar stays within this range. Though it is not admitting it, the Bank is following a fixed exchange-rate policy.

Many had predicted that a free-trade agreement would increase the flow of foreign capital into Canada, thereby pushing the dollar up by a few cents. But this does not explain the steep rise that occurred. For an explanation, one must look to the Bank of Canada rate, which determines the rates at which all money is lent within Canada. Historically this rate has stayed two to three percentage points above the U.S. central-bank rate, the Federal Reserve rate. At the end of 1987 the gap was $2\frac{3}{4}$ points. It widened throughout 1988. By the end of the year, as the trade deal was about to be implemented, the gap was 5 points. By the end of 1989 it was $5\frac{1}{2}$ points; halfway through 1990 it peaked at $7\frac{1}{2}$ points before falling back to $4\frac{1}{2}$ points.

So the Bank of Canada–engineered interest-rate hike was the main factor responsible for driving up the Canadian dollar; and the correlation between the signing of the free-trade agreement and the implementation of the high-interest-rate policy is compelling. It is not hard to imagine the Canadian government, desperate for an agreement that Brian Mulroney had publicly staked his political future on, making a secret exchange-rate deal.

(Although most such deals are now fronted by the International Monetary Fund, the Americans have directly imposed at least one exchange-rate pact on a foreign government. Recently declassified papers of former president Lyndon Johnson reveal that in 1964 they forced the ailing British Labour government to keep British troops in the Far East, to bring in wage and price controls, and not to devalue its currency for three years in return for propping

up the pound. British economic packages and budget proposals were vetted through the White House before being
shown to the British cabinet.)

The U.S. manufacturers' association, which had been
pushing hard for an exchange pact as part of the free-trade
negotiations, mysteriously withdrew its demand at the last
minute. What was their price for backing off? Interestingly, at the outset of the trilateral round of negotiations to extend free trade to Mexico, the National Association of Manufacturers once again asked the Bush
administration for assurances that any "new agreement
seek to prevent exchange-rate manipulation for a country's competitive advantage." A spokesman for the association stressed that it didn't have to be a formal
mechanism.

Whether or not the Conservative government made a
secret commitment to jack up the Canadian dollar, its
high–interest/exchange-rate policy is deliberate. It is
dramatically increasing the pace of harmonization and
restructuring and, in the process, ravaging the Canadian
economy. David Abramson, editor of the *International
Bank Credit Analyst*, sees it as a deliberate strategy to
discipline firms to cut wages and other costs — or fail.
"The ones remaining are the ones that can really
compete."

The exchange-rate issue is extremely important. During the free-trade debate, the government and free-trade
supporters told us that the exchange rate was the key safety
valve that would offset the harmonization pressures critics
were warning against. If Canadian cost structures, such as
wages and taxes, were too high in the newly integrated
market, they told us, the Canadian dollar would fall relative to the U.S. dollar. This would make Canadian costs
fall and nullify the original competitive disadvantage. Of

course, that did not happen. As the trade barriers came down and the markets moved closer together, the dollar rose rapidly, almost from the day the deal was signed.

The Role of the Free-Trade Agreement

The free-trade agreement is the bedrock of the Conservative/corporate agenda to reshape Canada as part of a new continental order. This new order is about shifting power from governments to corporations. It is about limiting the capacity of Canadian governments, present and future, to actively determine the course of economic development. It is about breaking down the structures of the national economy and preventing Canada from establishing an activist industrial policy, ever.

The Conservative view of industrial policy begins and ends with free trade; the role of government is to get out of the way after eliminating the barriers separating the two markets. Let the corporations wrestle free of public control in the mud of the newly created continental market, and let the losers go under.

The corporate survivors of this restructuring binge would be battle-hardened, able to compete in the global economy. The surviving work-force would be productive, "co-operative," and lower paid. In this new continental world, all distinctive features would be eroded to create a harmonized and Americanized playing field.

In the brave new world of free trade, Brian Mulroney promised us prosperity. When? "Soon after the agreement comes into effect," Michael Wilson assured us. There was a disturbing vagueness about these promises but Canadians took their leap of faith. Not to worry. This restructuring would be painless, the economy would grow. Jobs would be created — good jobs, highly skilled jobs. Every region, every province, every sector — workers, consumers, men, and women — everyone would benefit. There would be massive adjustment programs available should workers lose their jobs in the transition; however, as there would be no down side to free trade, they wouldn't be necessary.

There was one mote in this otherwise rosy vision. Buried deep in the 1985 International Trade Department report, *How to Secure and Enhance Our Export Markets*, was a single reference to the potential magnitude of adjustment to free trade. It estimated in bland technocratic language that "job dislocation" or "inter-industry employment shifts" would affect 7 percent of the work-force. The report was telling us, translated into plain English, that the transition to free trade would cost 850,000 jobs. (Had the specifics of the deal been known, the estimate would undoubtedly have been much higher.)

This slip was never repeated. Shortly thereafter, the Tories put into place their public-relations strategy to sell free trade. We heard nothing more of the potential down side, any more than the government admits that living with free trade for almost three years has meant upheaval for hundreds of thousands of workers and their families, for thousands of business people and their families, and for hundreds of Canadian communities.

The free-trade agreement is a complex legal document. It has direct and indirect effects, some clear and some obscure. It acts upon and reinforces existing policies; it gives rise to new policies of privatization, deregulation, taxation, social-program cutbacks, etc. It produces effects that generate secondary effects that cause still further effects. The ripples of causality are cumulative, fragmenting the national economy, removing the glue that holds together its constituent parts, and transforming it through restructuring and harmonization. Here are few examples to illustrate how it works.

The Free-Trade Agreement and the Auto Pact
The auto industry is critical to the Canadian economy. For every job created in this sector, five jobs are created elsewhere in the economy — in steel, textiles, glass, plastics, chemicals, and services. It accounts for one-half of our manufacturing exports to the United States. Much of our trade with the United States is governed by the terms of the Auto Pact, which the Tories held up as a successful example of free trade. That, of course, is nonsense. The Auto Pact is an example of managed trade, of how we worked out an arrangement with a foreign-dominated industry to ensure benefits to the Canadian economy. The pact has built-in safeguards to ensure that certain levels of production and jobs remain in Canada. The basic principle of the Auto Pact is that if a corporation is going to sell in the Canadian market, it must produce in that market.

The Tories have said they protected the Auto Pact within the FTA. They lied. Yes, they preserved the form, but they removed the substance. Most important, they removed the main enforcement mechanism, the tariffs. Without a penalty for breaking the rules, what is to keep the American auto companies from breaking their commitments? What will happen when it is more profitable to assemble vehicles or make components in Tennessee or Mexico? The Japanese manufacturers, which now have almost 40 percent of the Canadian market, have not been required by this or past governments to adhere to the Auto Pact. Consequently their commitment to Canadian production has been weak. If the Big Three were to match the Japanese commitment, they would be employing only 20,000 instead of 150,000 Canadian workers. Under the FTA, the Japanese have been prevented from being required to join the Auto Pact. Now that the pact has been defanged, they have only to meet a North American-content requirement to get duty-free access. That means, for example, that Nissan can export cars duty-free to Canada from its U.S. factories without being obliged to create a single manufacturing job here.

The consequences of eroding the Auto Pact have been dramatic. With the market now almost unchecked and the huge rise in the dollar pushing up costs, auto-parts companies are leaving Canada in droves. In two years of free trade, the Canadian auto-parts sector lost almost one-quarter of its production and almost one-fifth of its jobs. Plants are moving to the southern United States, where wages are $5 an hour and unions don't exist, or farther south, to the Mexican *maquiladora*, the border export zone where wages are 60 cents an hour.

One of the deserters was Shellar Globe, a big U.S.-owned auto-parts company. It closed its steering-wheel plant near Windsor, Ontario, rather than settle an eight-month strike. Its steering wheels are now made in Mexico. Kathy Kungel was one of the 350 workers who lost their jobs. She was earning $9.70 an hour. "Our lives have been devastated," she says. "Families have broken up. People have lost cars and homes. They wonder how they are going to feed and clothe their children. I now live back at home with my parents and my two kids. . . . Never in my life have I been on social services or taken handouts from anybody."

Where does Kathy Kungel fit into the new continental economy? She will be increasingly marginal, both as a consumer and as a producer. Like millions of Canadians, Kathy Kungel is expendable in the continental corporate order.

In nearby Chatham, the giant Motor Wheel Corp. told its 550 employees in January 1991 that, in order to stay competitive, it needed to cut wages and benefits from $26 an hour to $13 an hour. Otherwise, it would move south. "Would you take half your salary?" asked eighteen-year veteran Bill Gammage. "With no guarantees? They could leave in six months." The workers refused Motor Wheel's offer. The plant shut down.

The current economic crisis has hit manufacturing-dependent border communities such as Windsor and Chatham particularly hard. According to Pam Ponds, director of the Unemployed Help Centre, the Windsor area has lost more jobs per capita than any other community in Ontario; forty plants closed in 1990.

Chatham Chamber of Commerce president Paul Sunnen says workers have to be prepared to take pay cuts or else "people in the world [who] are prepared to work for less . . . will get the jobs." But the loss of highly paid manufacturing jobs is damaging to the local retail economy. Development officers are trying to replace lost jobs by revitalizing the tourist industry; but, even where successful, these jobs pay half the wages of the jobs lost.

The lure of cross-border shopping is also hurting the retail sector. Jay Smith, a laid-off Siemens employee, is campaigning to keep jobs and consumption in the community. According to a *Windsor Star* report, he is persuading merchants to sign a petition calling for legislation to require profitable companies to stay put. He then puts their names in local workplaces on posters, urging workers not to cross-border shop. "People don't realize when they're shopping in the States what they're doing to the economy. . . . You need a bargain, [especially] when you're unemployed, but, Christ, you're affecting your chances of finding another job," says Smith.

The Automotive Parts Manufacturers' Association of Canada is pushing hard for widespread regulatory concessions in order to be competitive in the new continental market: lower taxes; weaker labour laws in such areas as pay equity, workers' compensation, health and safety laws; lower UI and health-care premiums, etc. They all have to be pushed down towards the lowest common denominator. That lowest-common-denominator magnet is the southern United States and the Mexican *maquiladora*, for that is where a big chunk of the once-Canadian industry is "restructuring and harmonizing" itself.

What's so attractive about the southern United States? Take the case of Canadian-owned auto-parts manufacturer, Tridon Ltd., which closed two profitable plants in Burlington, Ontario, in 1990, dumped 550 employees, and moved production to Tennessee. Tridon chairman Don Green, former Ontario Man of the Year, whose company received an estimated $9 million in government assistance funding, insists, "There comes a time when you can't keep putting money into a business any more." Green, who has just built a mansion in Burlington, reportedly at a cost of $2.5 million, blamed the move on the high dollar, social programs, and high wages.

Manufacturing wages are one-third lower in Tennessee. The state doesn't have a minimum wage, spends little on social programs, and doesn't collect personal income tax. Unions are not welcome there. As business recruiter Alf Barnette put it, "We don't care if you build bombs in our towns; just don't bring a union."

One of the ways Tennessee and other southern states keep unions weak and standards low is through "right to work" laws. These laws permit workers to opt out of certified unions and not pay dues while requiring the unions to represent them at the bargaining table. This incentive to "free riding" undermines the principle of collective bargaining and has sharply reduced the number of unionized workers.

Business analysts see free trade having a similar effect in Canada. D.C. MacCharles writes, in *Toronto Business*: "The threat of job loss due to increased competition may make union-management relations more co-operative. . . . With some luck governments will also respond and adapt their labour codes to allow for right-to-work laws and other measures which will reduce the high degree of rigidity in Canadian labour markets."

The welcome mat is out in Tennessee for Don Green and others like him. (There isn't much the state won't do to woo Canadian business. The governor personally intervened to fast-track Mr. Green's work visa.) Said assistant economic development commissioner Robert Parsons, "We understand what business needs to operate."

Other FTA Losers
The Canadian steel industry was supposed to be one of the winners under free trade. It had modernized in the early 1980s; it was competitive; and was itching to get into the U.S. market. The FTA was supposed to give it protection against harassment under U.S. trade laws. How times have changed. The soaring dollar has blunted Canadian steel's competitive edge. Its customers in the auto and appliance industries are failing or fleeing. Far from making inroads into the American market, they are fighting off U.S. imports, which have increased their share of the Canadian market from 2 to 20 percent in the last three years.

At the same time, U.S. producers have been using their trade laws to obstruct Canadian steelmakers trying to export into the American market. Both Sydney Steel in Nova Scotia and Algoma Steel in Ontario have been hit hard by countervailing duties; both are on the verge of collapse. Even industry executives are publicly admitting that the much-vaunted dispute-settlement mechanism is not working the way it was supposed to.

The food-processing industry is Canada's largest employer. Production is distributed widely across the country. It has been shaped by long-standing policies of national security of food supply and by policies of supply management, through commodities-marketing boards, which balance supply and demand and provide stable farm incomes with the help of tariffs and quotas.

Under this system, quality food is produced at reasonable prices. (Canadians pay on average about the same portion of their incomes on food as do Americans.) It provides processing jobs and makes farms secure. The main flaw is insufficient controls on the giant food processors and retailers, which have tended to gouge both the consumer and the farmer.

The free-trade agreement has radically altered food production in Canada. In the first two years of the new corporate free-for-all, the industry has lost 40,000 jobs. The fruit and vegetable farmers are caught in a disastrous double bind: the 15 to 20 percent tariffs on U.S. produce have been coming down and the protection of a low dollar has gone.

U.S. food conglomerate Hunt-Wesson shut down its ketchup plant in Tilbury, Ontario, and shifted production to its operations in Ohio and California. Farmer Doug Stockwell now has a half-million-dollar tomato farm and no buyer for his tomatoes. The company says Canada is too costly; cheaper labour and cheaper tomatoes are to be had south of the border. Stockwell says free trade has freed the company from its responsibility to buy and process in Canada for the Canadian market. They are both right.

Meanwhile, Hunt-Wesson increases its profits, Canadian workers lose their jobs, the Stockwell farm, like that of its neighbours, is "going down the drain," and Canada has lost even more food self-sufficiency.

In the clauses related to supply-managed sectors such as poultry and dairy, the Conservative government crafted the FTA to make it appear that supply management was left intact, but removed the means of making the system work. Imported processed foods such as ice cream and yoghurt used to be restricted by high tariffs. Under the FTA, U.S. companies, which use cheaper U.S milk, can ship their ice cream into the country tariff-free. Canadian processors have to use higher-priced Canadian milk in their ice cream. Factor in the high Canadian dollar, and it is clear our industry can't compete in Canada, let alone continent-wide. Eventually, supply management will die. Farms will go under, and many more people will lose their processing jobs. Then transition to continental corporate relations of agriculture will be complete.

The Canadian Wheat Board is an export monopoly, an instrument of power for Canadian grain farmers selling wheat in a world market dominated by five U.S. multinationals. Canadian grain prices are extremely low because the U.S. government is bankrolling an international grain war with the European community. Moreover, American grain is now flowing into Canada under provisions of the FTA and is undercutting the price of Canadian grain. The U.S. government is also subsidizing exports into foreign markets, in direct competition with Canadian exports, a direct violation of the FTA.

The undermining of the Wheat Board is but another nail in the coffin of a national economy, the triumph of raw market forces controlled by Cargill and the other giant merchants of grain.

Nabisco Inc. has major investments in Canada. It was a key free-trade supporter, one of the largest contributors to Brian Mulroney's election campaign in 1988. It was also the president of Nabisco Canada who advised his corporate colleagues, shortly after the election, to use free trade to "mobilize employees to cut costs." "Nothing," he said, "clears the mind so much as the spectre of being hung in the morning." Nabisco is putting its free-trade noose to work. In early January 1991, it forced employees at its Niagara Falls plant out on strike by demanding wide-ranging contract concessions such as mandatory overtime. Why? So the company can compete in a free-trade market, replied company officials. Several weeks into the strike, Nabisco closed their plant in nearby Simcoe. Coincidence or intimidation? Harmonization in action.

Unlike the food industry, Canadian clothing companies were in trouble before the Conservatives came to power, fighting to survive against imports from third-world countries. While output stayed steady through the 1980s, it lost market share and 15 percent of its work-force. But, two years into free trade, output dropped 15 percent and 18,000 workers (20 percent of the industry) lost their jobs. The industry has had to deal with the rising dollar and the removal of tariffs; but more devastating is the large U.S. companies' advantage of producing much of the labour-intensive work duty-free in the Mexican *maquiladora*, for 55 cents an hour. Clothing may be a vital commodity, but the Canadian industry is expendable in the new continental economy.

The clothing industry is labour-intensive, concentrated in Montreal, Toronto, and Winnipeg. It employs mainly women, immigrants, and older workers with little schooling. Nota Havaris is fifty-eight years old. She came to

Canada from Greece thirty-four years ago and always worked for one employer, J.H. Warsh & Co., one of Canada's oldest apparel manufacturers. A highly skilled worker, she earned $12.63 an hour. She was putting her daughter through the University of Toronto engineering school.

J.H. Warsh began laying off staff in 1989, when its licence to make Anne Klein clothing was revoked; with the tariffs coming off, the American manufacturer could now supply the line for Canada more cheaply from its factories in the United States. On December 5, 1990, J.H. Warsh went bankrupt. Nota received no severance pay, nor does she qualify for the Conservatives' new Program for Older Worker Adjustment (POWA) — only a tiny fraction of laid-off older workers qualify for assistance under its tight eligibility rules. Under the Tories' new, tight-fisted policy, Nota can collect unemployment-insurance benefits for only thirty-five weeks instead of one full year. After that, welfare? Her daughter has had to suspend her university studies.

Selling Out Canada, Wholesale
Paradoxically, as free trade has driven companies out of business or south of the border, it has also cleared the way for American companies to resume their wholesale buyout of the Canadian economy. The Conservatives began to deregulate U.S. corporate activity in 1985 by killing the Foreign Investment Review Agency and replacing it with Investment Canada. Its mandate is not really to review corporate takeovers but to hold open the door. In six years of operation it has allowed more than 4,000 Canadian-based companies to be taken over by foreign-owned corporations. It has not turned down a single application.

The free-trade agreement ensured that no future government could reregulate foreign corporations doing business in Canada. The vestiges of the regulatory framework left in place are unenforceable.

One of the 4,000 foreign takeovers of Canadian-based companies that Investment Canada approved was that of Varta Batteries, by its major competitor, the giant auto-parts maker Johnson Controls Inc. of Milwaukee. The takeover gave Johnson control of 75 percent of the Canadian auto-battery market. In January 1990, two weeks after the takeover was approved, Johnson announced that it was closing Varta's Winnipeg plant, putting 192 employees out of work; only Varta's St. Thomas plant would be left operating. A year later, Johnson Controls shut down another Canadian plant, in Port Perry, Ontario. Production moved to Tennessee and 280 Canadian workers lost their jobs.

Johnson owns scores of low-wage, non-unionized auto-parts plants scattered throughout the southern United States and the *maquiladora* region of Mexico. There are no compelling reasons for Johnson Controls to remain in Canada.

As for the laid-off Varta employees in Winnipeg, at last count only 30 of the 160 shop-floor staff had found other jobs, but few at comparable wages. Unemployment insurance is fast running out, after which there is only welfare. Aleem Chaudary has applied for many jobs, but opportunities are scarce and the competition is fierce. He is trying to get government financial support, so far unsuccessfully, to go back to the local community college. His future in the new continental economy, like that of Winnipeg itself, is precarious.

The free-trade–driven continentalization of the Canadian

economy is tearing at the national transportation/communication infrastructure, the steel, concrete, fibre-optic, and aerial ribbons that tie our economy together along the forty-ninth parallel. Regions are becoming rapidly disconnected as the national economy breaks down into "five regional economies that are increasingly trading along separate north-south axes with the United States," as accounting firm Coopers & Lybrand said in its report *Reshaping Canada to Compete.*

Perhaps none is more visibly torn than the trucking sector. Almost half a million Canadians are employed in this industry; three-quarters of the goods traded between Canada and the United States are carried by truck.

On the day the Mulroney government signed the trade deal it also passed a law deregulating the transportation system. Under the FTA, American companies were assured equal access to the newly deregulated market, even though U.S. state laws prevent Canadian companies from having the same access to the American market.

A small group of giants dominate the U.S. trucking industry. Survivors of earlier deregulation, they dwarf the Canadian competition. These mega-carriers stormed into Canada armed with the advantage of lower costs on everything from wages to insurance, fuel, taxes, and borrowing. This edge was estimated at about 20 percent, although the U.S. companies have been reportedly undercutting Canadian bids by as much as a third. (A 72-cent dollar would just about offset this disadvantage; but the Mulroney government would rather keep the dollar pegged at 86 cents and waste the Canadian industry.)

The "killing fields of bankruptcies," as one trucker described it, claimed 656 companies in 1990; 1991 looks worse. Desperate truckers all over the country are making last-ditch efforts to get the government's attention, snarling traffic at border crossings, on major highways, and in front of legislatures.

One protester, independent trucker Tom McMurdie, lost his rig because he could no longer earn enough to make the $3,000 monthly payment. Another, Greg Wolfendon, earned only $9,000 in 1990. He and his family are getting by only because of his wife's mother's allowance cheque.

The large Canadian companies have established bases in the United States and have transferred thousands of jobs. Before deregulation and free trade, Thompson Transport employed a staff of 640. In 1989, it laid off 250 drivers and office staff, cut its fleet from 475 to 175 tractors, and opened a branch in Detroit. Two years later it closed its Canadian base. Survival for Thompson meant becoming American.

The FTA prevents special treatment for Canadian companies. It prevents the exchange rate from falling. It prevents reregulation of the industry. Ironically, the truckers' protests for lower taxes is feeding into the very harmonization agenda that is destroying them; for lower taxes reduce the ability of government to provide education and health care and the other services that make Canadian society different from that of our neighbour.

The free-trade–driven transformation of the Canadian economy, Mulroney and the BCNI tell us, is about freedom. And they are right. It is entrenching the freedom of corporations to move production and technology wherever they want on the continent. It guarantees them the freedom to move executives' and workers' jobs, but not workers; the freedom to move profits and capital, and ship back into Canada without penalty.

It also, for practical purposes, is the freedom of Canadian consumers to shop anywhere on the continent and bring back their purchases without restriction. The number of Canadian shoppers crossing the border is so high it is bleeding the country of billions of dollars in sales, of millions of tax dollars, of thousands of jobs, and of hundreds of businesses. It is also deliberate government policy.

During the free-trade debate, the Tories promised lower prices for Canadian consumers. What they meant, it turns out, was higher prices for Canadians buying in Canada and lower prices for Canadians buying in the United States. First, they raised the dollar, which lowered the cost of purchases in the United States; second, they raised the dollar limits on what Canadians could bring back and reduced surveillance at the border. The government even set up a fast lane for regular shoppers: to avoid border delays, just drop your customs claims in a slot and pay the duty later, by mail. Surely the day is not far off when the border will be redundant.

Third, to force the provinces to harmonize their sales-tax schedules with the GST, the Conservatives have refused to collect provincial sales taxes at the border. This policy will cost "unco-operative" provinces an estimated $200 million and 30,000 jobs.

When the beleaguered border towns appealed to the government to level their playing field, trade minister John Crosbie told them, "Get off your duffs and compete." Indeed. But as Kim Carter of the Canadian Council of Grocery Distributors put it, "We have a mixed economy that is trying to compete against a market-driven economy." What chance has the mixed economy when the rules of the game are market rules, and when the market economy is ten times its size? The market economy floods over the border. How long can our mixed economy tread water?

Pity John Bulloch, president of the Canadian Federation of Independent Business, the largest organization of small- and medium-sized businesses in Canada. Unlike boat manufacturer Peter Francis, Bulloch believed the line spun by big business and the Mulroney government about free trade. The locker-room bravado of "we can compete" and the promise of "getting the government off our backs" was too much for him to resist. The CFIB was too dazzled by visions of sugar plums to do a serious analysis of how the trade deal would affect its members. It even bought the government line that the dollar wouldn't rise.

Even as thousands of his members have gone under, Mr. Bulloch is still a believer. He slams the government for the havoc its high interest rates are causing, but he vehemently denies that free trade has anything to do with the havoc. "Competitiveness is the issue," he chants. Interest rates and taxes are the impediments. He still can't see that free trade has everything to do with interest rates and taxes and competitiveness.

He should listen to Trevor Eyton, CEO of the Bronfman group's Brascan and GST senator, who said that free trade was a necessary step in the "quest for competitiveness." Unlike John Bulloch's small-business members, who are the cannon-fodder of the embattled Canadian economy, free trade is Brascan's membership card to the new borderless world economy.

2.

THE CONTINENTAL SELLOUT

"Poor Mexico — so far from God and so close to the United States."

— Old Mexican saying

WHEN BRIAN MULRONEY WENT TO MEXICO in March 1990 with representatives from the BCNI, he was asked by reporters what he thought about Mexico becoming part of the Canada-U.S. Free Trade Agreement. He coyly responded that he "wouldn't be scandalized" by the prospect. This was the first official indication that extending the trade deal to Mexico was under serious consideration by the Canadian government.

Two weeks later, *The Wall Street Journal* reported that the Mexican and U.S. governments were about to enter formal free-trade negotiations. This was the first time the Mexican public had heard of such talks. President Carlos Salinas de Gortari spoke effusively of the benefits free trade had brought to Canada. "It created 250,000 jobs," he said. "Industry did not collapse as they said it would. Foreign investment increased. Exports increased." It was obvious who was feeding him this misinformation. Two and a half months later, on June 11, presidents Bush and Salinas formally announced their intent to negotiate a free-trade deal.

On September 25, the day President Bush asked Congress for fast-track negotiating authority, trade minister John Crosbie announced that Canada was requesting full participation in these negotiations. The Conservatives made this decision without consulting Parliament and without public hearings. They did, however, consult the International Trade Advisory Committee (ITAC), chaired by Brascan head and GST senator-to-be Trevor Eyton.

Only months earlier Crosbie had publicly denied that Canada was interested in entering into a trade deal with Mexico, although all the signs said otherwise. In the fall of 1989, the government reversed a long-standing policy and committed Canada to full membership in the Organization of American States. Canada had, in the past, avoided this American-dominated forum because of the danger of becoming hostage to U.S. foreign policies. This was clearly not a concern for Brian Mulroney. The same month, the Canadian embassy in Washington and the Royal Bank of Canada jointly sponsored a conference in El Paso, Texas, called "Region North America." Many of the Canadian and American technocrats who negotiated the FTA were there, plugging the benefits of a continental accord.

The Conservative government knew before it signed the FTA that the Americans wanted a continental deal. Reagan had talked about a common market from "the Yukon to the Yucatan" as early as 1980. Bush had repeated this commitment during his 1988 election campaign. Canadian negotiators had even tried, unsuccessfully, to insert a clause in the FTA that would prevent the United States from playing Canada and Mexico off against each other by ensuring that any benefits extended to one would automatically be given to the other.

On the day President Bush announced his intention to negotiate a free-trade agreement with Mexico, he revealed that it was part of a much larger plan to create a giant free-trade area from "the Arctic Circle to Tierra del Fuego." He called it the Enterprise for the Americas Initiative.

The goal is to free up the flow of goods, services, and capital for U.S. transnational corporate interests, to limit the power of governments, to deregulate, and to privatize. The Canada-U.S. Free Trade Agreement is the model, setting out the basic rules to be extended throughout the hemisphere.

The carrot dangled before Latin American governments is a promise of some small relief from their crippling foreign debts, and access to the U.S. market. Bush has promised a $300-million fund to facilitate privatization. This is an extension of "structural adjustment" programs imposed on Latin American governments by its surrogates, the International Monetary Fund and the World Bank.

Mexico is crucial to the Enterprise for the Americas project. The corporate community brought out its heavy Washington artillery to ensure that the U.S. Congress gave President Bush the "fast track" negotiating authority to conclude a Mexican deal. This time, however, resistance within the United States is much greater than it was during negotiations with Canada. Labour, farm, environment, and other popular organizations face a much greater threat from Mexican free trade and have put together a strong opposition.

Corporate America mobilized a 500-member, ad hoc lobby called the Coalition for Trade Expansion. Most of the players who pushed through the Canada-U.S. deal are part of the coalition, as it includes the heads of virtually every major business organization, from the Business Round Table to the National Association of Manufacturers. It includes all the major corporations: American Express, AT&T, Coca-Cola, Exxon, Ford, General Electric, General Motors, IBM, Zenith, Kodak, and many more. It also includes the major lobbyists. Thomas Enders, former ambassador to Canada and U.S. under-secretary for Latin America, leads the Mexico-U.S. Business Committee. Former vice-president of American Express Harry Freeman is a consultant to the coalition. So are former U.S. trade representatives Robert Strauss, a Democrat, and William Brock, a Republican.

The Enterprise for the Americas agenda is moving quickly. The United States has already signed framework trade agreements, precursors to formal free-trade negotiations, with Chile, Colombia, Ecuador, and Bolivia. It is currently negotiating framework agreements with Venezuela and Costa Rica. It is also negotiating jointly with Brazil, Argentina, and Uruguay, who are themselves moving towards a common market.

The Enterprise for the Americas Initiative is part of George Bush's re-energized American drive "to unashamedly lay down the rules of world order," as foreign-policy analyst Charles Krauthammer puts it. This is a far cry from the new world order of the 1980 Brandt Commission or the 1969 U.N. commission headed by Lester Pearson, which envisaged a more just and peaceful world wherein the cruel inequities of the third world were reduced.

Bush's New World Order is based on the raw exercise of economic might and military supremacy. The brutality of the Gulf War illustrates just how far the United States is prepared to go. It was, as Bush himself put it, "the first test of the new order," securing the dominance of U.S. corporations over the world's two largest industries, oil and arms. Since the Gulf War, the United States has sold more than $13 billion worth of arms to five Middle Eastern countries. "The peace dividend is replaced by a war dividend, the disarmament-development agenda eclipsed by resurgent militarism," says Douglas Roche, Canada's former ambassador for disarmament.

The Enterprise for the Americas Initiative is an attempt to lock into its imperial orbit a bloc of satellite nations over which U.S. economic dominance is undisputed. The U.S. economy is larger by far than the combined economies of all thirty-four nations of the Americas. The initiative is part of another U.S. war effort, the war to re-establish its waning economic superiority.

The U.S. government is the trustee and executor of U.S. corporate interests world-wide. The Mulroney government has chosen to be a loyal cheerleader to U.S. foreign-policy initiatives in exchange for the façade of being an important insider.

The 600 largest transnational corporations account for one-quarter of the world's total output. Ownership is concentrated in the United States and a handful of other countries. They do 80 to 90 percent of the industrial world's trade, but employ just 3 percent of the world's work-force; two-thirds of these employees are located in the home countries. Transnationals are economic fiefdoms: flexible, dynamic, and autocratic. Their goals are to survive, to grow, and to accumulate wealth. They operate in national jurisdictions around the world, but are able to circumvent, and therefore weaken, national jurisdictions.

Their defining characteristic is that they have internalized the market. What is produced, where each stage of the process is to be produced, at what prices goods and services are exchanged among the parts of the corporation, where to locate R&D, how to allocate tax burdens — all of these decisions are under the control of the executives at the corporate headquarters. The transnationals, unlike the failed totalitarian state experiments, are successful examples of centrally managed production and trade. One half of all the world's trade takes place as transactions within these corporations, rather than in the open market.

And it is these global behemoths that are the *raison d'être* of U.S. government policies of free trade.

South of the Border

"Money has no heart, no soul, no conscience, no homeland." Thus Frank Stronach, chairman of the Canadian auto-parts manufacturer Magna International Inc., announced his company's intention to set up a joint venture in the *maquiladora* to make bumpers for Volkswagen. Frank Stronach was another of those rare businessmen who opposed the free-trade agreement, not because he doubted that his company could survive, but because he doubted whether Canada could survive. He knew that free trade with the United States included its "back door," the *maquiladora*. This, combined with the evisceration of the Auto Pact, could be disastrous for the Canadian industry.

Stronach vowed in 1988 that he would not move business to Mexico if the free-trade agreement did not come to pass.

Today Magna is facing hard times, free trade, and a huge debt load in the midst of a deep recession and Stronach is resigned to the inevitability of a North American common market.

Stronach is a latecomer to Mexico. All the major auto makers are there already, and so are the major parts manufacturers.

The *maquiladora* is a partial free-trade zone strapped to the underbelly of the United States. It hugs 3,000 km of arid Mexican-U.S. border across two mountain ranges, from Tijuana on the Pacific coast just below San Diego to Matamoros on the Rio Grande, just below Brownsville, Texas. In between are another half-dozen centres of *maquiladora* production: Mexicali, Laredo, Nogales, Ciudad Juárez, and Reynosa.

Since the early 1980s, the *maquiladora* has been a focal point of activity for American transnational corporations. There are now more than 2,000 plants operating in the zone, twice as many as there were five years ago. They are part of almost every manufactured item we buy: from televisions to cars, from washing machines to toaster ovens, from clothing to computers. They employ half a million Mexican workers, four times the work-force of ten years ago. By mid-decade they will employ more than a million. A million and a half Mexicans have come from the interior, swelling the border communities to the breaking point.

The transnationals are bringing the first world and the third world into one unified continental economy. The collision is causing unparalleled social and economic upheaval in both worlds. As production shifts south, plants have closed in communities across the United States and Canada, and hundreds of thousands of people have lost their jobs.

The Fortune 500 corporations dominate the *maquiladora* landscape: General Motors, Ford, Chrysler, General Electric, IBM, Black and Decker, Westinghouse, Zenith, IT&T, Kodak, Campbell Soup, Whirlpool (Inglis), Allied Signal (Bendix), Du Pont, etc. European and Japanese transnationals are also there: Toyota, Nissan, Sony, Hitachi, Sanyo, Canon, Pioneer, Volkswagen, Unilever, Philips. Taiwanese and Korean transnationals, such as Samsung and Goldstar, are moving in. Canadian companies are arriving: Mitel, Northern Telecom, Fleck, Custom Trim.

The few Mexican companies that participate in *maquiladora* production do so as subcontractors for the foreign corporations. Most of the older industry of the area, industry that produced basic goods such as clothing, beer, and foodstuffs, has retreated into the interior or has been transformed to fit the new economic reality of the border.

The *maquiladora*, despite its profound dislocating effects, is, paradoxically, an isolated enclave. The foreign companies bring in their components from the United States or elsewhere, use cheap Mexican labour to assemble or otherwise transform them, and ship the processed goods back to an external market almost entirely in the United States and Canada. The Mexican-made content of *maquiladora* products is less than 2 percent; less than 2 percent of *maquiladora* production is consumed within Mexico.

Why has the *maquiladora* become such a powerful magnet for the corporations? The lodestone is wages that are among the lowest in the world — a quarter of those in Singapore or Korea, even lower than wages in Haiti. As one entrepreneur put it: "It's a businessman's dream."

When the international debt crisis hit in 1982, Mexico, like other Latin American countries, got caught in a squeeze between soaring international interest rates, plunging oil prices, and a lending freeze by Western banks. The result was internal chaos and the collapse of its currency. The Mexican peso, which traded at 25 to the U.S. dollar before the crisis, hit 1,500 to the dollar within the year and continued to slide downward throughout the 1980s. The peso now trades at close to 3,000 to the dollar.

The result was an enormous drop in Mexican wages in U.S.-dollar terms. Before the collapse, wages averaged $11 per day. By 1990 they were $4.50 per day. This was a windfall for the U.S. transnationals, which were struggling to regain the economic dominance they were losing to the Japanese. Indeed, the explosive growth of the *maquiladora* would not have been possible without the drop in Mexican wages.

The external financial crisis forced a desperate Mexico to go to the International Monetary Fund, which agreed to a series of loans — on onerous conditions. Mexico was required to take Draconian measures: restrictive monetary policies; huge government-spending cuts, particularly to social subsidies; wage controls; price deregulation; privatization; and trade liberalization. Mexico has assiduously taken the IMF medicine and implemented "structural adjustment programs" and, unlike many third-world patients, is considered to be doing well.

Celebrated Peruvian novelist Mario Vargas Llosa called Mexico "the perfect dictatorship." The PRI party has ruled the country for sixty years. Behind its façade of democracy, it maintains, as the Inter-Church Committee for Human Rights in Latin America observes, "control of virtually all aspects of Mexican society."

When the political opposition threatens to take power, as Cuauthemoc Cárdenas did in the 1988 presidential election against Carlos Salinas, the PRI uses its control of the electoral system — there is no independent electoral commission — and the legal system — there is no independent judiciary — to gerrymander the vote and declare itself the victor. The PRI controls brutal military and police forces, which routinely torture and murder political and labour opposition. According to the 1990 report of the human-rights group Americas Watch, "Recent events portend that rather than moving towards improvements in human rights conditions, Mexico may be heading for a period of increased violent abuses and suppression of dissent."

So effective was Mexico's IMF-approved "structural adjustment" that, by the end of 1989, wages in Mexico had fallen to one-half their 1981 levels. Wage income shrank from 40 to 28 percent of national income; during the same period, employers increased their share from 48 to 65 percent. (Reagan and Mulroney policies were eating away at wages in the United States and Canada, but they were not able to achieve anything remotely close to the wage compression that occurred in Mexico during the 1980s.)

The key elements in the formula for keeping *maquiladora* wages at rock bottom, therefore, have been an imploding currency and a government that smothers political opposition and suppresses independent worker movements, brutally if necessary.

In a number of *maquiladora* cities, such as Matamoros, government-sanctioned unions control virtually the entire labour force. In others, such as Tijuana, the unions are less powerful, controlling only a third of the work-force. Most Mexican unions are part of government apparatus: to be a union member is to have automatic membership in the PRI party. Union leadership is allocated a large block of seats in the national legislature.

But these are not independent unions as we know them in Canada. Unions in the *maquiladora* are means of maintaining labour peace for the companies, not a force for improving wages and working conditions for their members. Union leaders are brokers in human labour. They are sometimes a nuisance to the companies, and they have to be paid for their services; many companies pursue a deliberate policy of keeping unions out. Nevertheless, they are a necessary part of the structure that keeps wages low.

Maquiladora workers, two-thirds of whom are women, have been described as "unspoiled labour." Companies hire and fire at will and weed out unproductive or troublesome workers. Women are routinely dismissed when they become pregnant. The burn-out rate is five to ten years, and very few last past the age of twenty-five.

Despite the huge influx of people into the border region, there is full employment. "Help wanted" signs are everywhere, and it is not uncommon for a facility to see its entire work-force turn over in a year. Nevertheless, wage levels remain uniformly low. Keith Bandolik, a *maquila* manager for the Chicago-based Switchcraft Corporation, explains: "Everybody keeps track of what everybody is paying. Everybody wants to keep wages down. If you defeat that you defeat your reason for being there." Maintaining low wages is facilitated by a glossy magazine for *maquiladora* operators called *Twin Plant News.* Articles suggest ways "to keep minimum-wage people at the minimum wage." They advise using a charity approach. Offer free or subsidized meals and transportation. U.S. companies, they say, could send unwanted clothes to their Mexican subsidiary, because "warm clothing and blankets feel good on those cold nights." However, these articles warn "don't throw good money after bad. . . if wages go past an acceptable level they will not cause more satisfaction . . . for the worker."

Low wages alone would not attract the world's transnational corporations to the Mexican *maquiladora*; but because companies are able to bring with them sophisticated industrial processes and equipment, workers are turning out quality goods at high levels of productivity. The traditional sweatshop still exists, but modern, efficient plants are increasingly the norm. Business guru and Claremont University professor Peter Drucker says, "It takes three years at the most for a *maquila* to attain the labour productivity of a well-run U.S. or Japanese plant, even turning out highly sophisticated products." The gains to the corporations from this high productivity at low wages are dramatic.

Central to the argument of Conservative, business, media, and academic proponents of free trade with Mexico is the myth that we don't have to worry about major job loss in Canada because worker productivity is so much lower in Mexico. This may be true for the Mexican economy as a whole; but it is far from true for the *maquiladora*, which is the threat to Canadian jobs and social standards.

There is a macho appeal in the briefs of the BCNI and the Bank of Montreal, in the editorials of *The Globe and Mail* and *The Financial Post*, not unlike what we heard during the original free-trade debate: We can compete, because we're more productive, more educated, more highly skilled, in short, because we're superior. This argument is a seductive but dangerous distortion of the reality that Canadian workers and companies face in an integrated continental economy.

This reality is described by Vancouver entrepreneur Jimmy Pattison in his autobiography. "I recently saw a new half-billion-dollar Ford factory that is the most automated car-manufacturing plant in the world. . . . Sixteen hundred Mexican workers, with no experience in the auto industry, operate the plant with no quality-control inspectors on site — and Ford is the industry leader in quality." Backing up the Hermosillo assembly plant Pattison describes is a stable of high-quality auto-parts suppliers in the *maquiladora*.

The Japanese also attest to the high productivity levels achievable in the *maquiladora*. Dr. Mitsuru Misawa, head of the foreign-investment department of the Industrial

Bank of Japan, made two striking observations after a tour of *maquiladora* plants: First, "though the labour costs were one-ninth the U.S. level, labour productivity was surprisingly higher than in the U.S."; and second, "though considerable efforts are required to set up a properly functioning system (an average of two years), once the system is in place the quality of the products is superior to those made in the U.S." *Maquiladora* production is central to the Japanese strategy of maintaining their access to the American market and staying competitive in the face of the steep appreciation of the yen.

So when *The Globe and Mail* says, "Mexican wages are low because the productivity of Mexican workers is low," it misinforms Canadians. When it dismissively says that "wages account for only a modest portion (18–20%) of direct manufacturing costs in Canada," it seems unaware that Peter Drucker sees a good case for moving to the *maquiladora* when wages are 15 percent or more of direct manufacturing costs. By Drucker's rule of thumb, more than half the Canadian manufacturing sector is at risk in an integrated continental economy.

The *maquiladora* also offers other advantages that reinforce the wage/productivity advantage. It exempts foreign corporations from Mexican laws requiring majority Mexican ownership. As long as they export the bulk of what they produce, they are allowed to be 100 percent foreign-owned. It also exempts the corporations from duties: on the imported materials to be worked on, on all but the value added by Mexican labour to exports to the United States. Taxes are low and easily avoidable; environmental regulations are weak and not enforced.

An essential advantage of the Mexican *maquiladora* is its location. Unlike most third world export-processing zones, it is on the doorstep of the American market; therefore it can make use of the U.S. transportation and communication infrastructure. Cross a bridge and your goods are immediately plugged into a sophisticated transportation grid that will get them to most American cities within thirty-six hours. Forty-eight hours and they are at the Ontario border. Furthermore, there are none of the problems usually encountered by relocated executives. They are not forced to raise their families in a distant country with strange customs and a foreign language. They can commute from San Diego or El Paso, Texas.

The Mexican-American Chamber of Commerce estimates that cost advantage of the average *maquiladora* plant over a comparable U.S. plant amounts to $13 per worker per hour. This represents a windfall profit of US$15–20 billion each year for the 2,000 *maquiladora* plants. A company cannot afford to ignore such competitive advantage in a deregulated market environment.

Touring in Juarez
Electrowire Inc. is a U.S.-owned company that makes electrical harnesses for automobiles. The facility employs 1,000 workers, average age eighteen. The plant's main customer is the Ford Motor plant in St. Thomas, Ontario. So tightly is production integrated to its Canadian customer that, when the CAW went on strike for a week in September, it also shut down.

This is a state-of-the-art facility. Productivity is comparable with that of Electrowire Canada Inc., in Owen Sound, Ontario.

During the last contract negotiations, the Canadian company demanded many concessions and offered a 3 percent wage increase over three years. To encourage the union, the company produced a letter from a firm that helps companies set up shop in the *maquiladora*. The letter boasted about the advantages of "cooperative workers that follow your instructions" and "hourly costs including bonuses, space and utilities from $2.95 to $4.50, as compared with Canadian costs of $13.00, which don't include these extras." The workers capitulated to the company's demands. Nevertheless, the future looks bleak; only one hundred are still working in a plant that employed four hundred a decade ago.

Carmen works at the Electrowire plant in Juarez. She is eighteen. For a forty-eight-hour week she makes $25, less $5 for transportation. She gets up at 4:00 AM to make her six o'clock shift. She receives a free meal at work; but food and water for her and her two-and-a-half-year-old son cost $15 per week. Carmen lives with her mother and eight-year-old sister in a squatters' community on the outskirts of Juarez. The one-room shack of corrugated tin has no sewage. The eight-year-old takes care of Carmen's child while she is at work.

Carmen has worked in the *maquiladora* for almost four years. Her pay hasn't changed much, but each year it buys less and less. She feels a growing sense of despair but clings to the hope that somehow life will be better for her son.

For Canadians, the *maquiladora* is a tour of jobs lost. The Bermudez industrial park is the world's largest, employing 35,000 people. Corporations producing there include General Motors, Outboard Marine, Cooper Industries, and United Technologies. All have laid off workers and closed plants in Canada in the last two years.

A Ford worker says that a group of Canadian managers recently visited his plant. Ford was relocating the seat production of its Crown Victoria and Mercury Marquis cars. The move cost 140 Canadian workers their jobs.

Some of the work done at a TRW Inc. seat-belt factory in Reynosa used to be done by Bendix in Collingwood,

Ontario; it closed in 1990, putting four hundred people out of work. Johnson Controls produces batteries in Reynosa. Some of its production used to be done at its now defunct Varta plant in Winnipeg.

Enrique works at Kimberly-Clark factory in Nogales. He makes hospital gowns for $35 a week. Sixty workers at Bovie Manufacturing in Lindsay, Ontario, lost their jobs in 1989 when the company lost the main contract to make hospital gowns for Kimberly-Clark. The contract went to Mexico. (The head of Kimberly-Clark Mexico is a special trade adviser to Mexican president Carlos Salinas.) Fleck Manufacturing, the company that closed down a striking plant in Centralia, Ontario, during the 1988 election, has also relocated in Nogales.

The Toxic Playing Field
Dr. Roberto Sanchez of the Colegio de la Frontera Norte has conducted extensive interviews of companies operating in the *maquiladora*. He has found that almost one company in five admits that the lack of environmental regulation was an important factor in its decision to locate there. (This finding is confirmed by the extensive research of Leslie Kochan of the Oregon Department of Environmental Quality.)

Take the California furniture industry. Companies have been fleeing across the border to Tijuana in order to escape a 1988 state law that imposes strict environmental controls on the release of fumes from solvent-based paints, stains, and lacquers. In Mexico they can not only pollute but also avoid workers' compensation premiums. Ironically, the pollution that the California law sought to eliminate still goes into the atmosphere a few miles south. Mexican workers are endangering their health through exposure to cancer-causing chemicals, American workers are unemployed, and California is under pressure to lower environmental standards to keep jobs.

The Automotive Parts Manufacturers' Association of Canada cites stringent Ontario workplace health and safety laws as one cause of their decreasing competitiveness. The industry pressured the Peterson government to withdraw proposed higher standards; the pressure can only intensify on the NDP.

Nine out of ten U.S. companies in the *maquiladora* work with toxic materials. By law they are supposed to return the waste to the United States for disposal; only 2 percent do. There in no environmental enforcement in Mexico. Ciudad Juárez alone is thought to generate 5,000 tons of toxic waste each year; most of it is dumped illegally.

The American Medical Association calls the border region "a virtual cesspool." In Tijuana, toxic waste dumped by plants in an industrial park forms a black bubbling lagoon. Where it meets untreated raw sewage, it turns into a small stream that runs past squatters' camps, in which children covered in sores drink Pepsi-Cola from baby bottles. It then empties into the Tijuana River.

In the plants, young women work with no protective covering beside open vats of toxic waste. Irma Olivia Garcia describes her working conditions: "At Mexon Surgical Supplies the silicone made my hands so sore my sister-in-law had to do my wash. I switched to VideoTec, but the acetone gave me anemia. . . . You should see the women coming out of Matsushita, where they do welding under a microscope. Their eyes look so bad we call them *marijuaneras.*"

Local newspaper headlines routinely record the environmental danger that is part of life in the *maquiladora.* "Special Education Supervisor Links Birth Defects to

Chemical Exposure in the Maquiladoras"; "Trico Corporation — 36 Workers Overcome in Gas Leak"; "General Motors Denounced for Discharging Chemicals into Canal"; "Zenith Electronics — 100 Workers Overcome by Fumes During Toxic Chemical Accident"; "Retzloff Chemical Accident Sends Chemical Cloud over City: Hundreds Overcome by Fumes."

Why does the Mexican government not take measures to enforce environmental standards? As one official told a U.S. trade department inquiry into North American free trade, "Mexico does not want industries that pollute, but we must remain competitive. That is why we don't push environmental enforcement."

Maquiladora North?

Is the *maquiladora* a distant mirror of Canada in a world of continental free trade? Certainly there are Canadians who live in conditions not much different from those in Mexico. Their numbers are small, but growing. Certainly, restructuring and harmonization are pushing down wages and standards. Social supports are weakening, and the government is not redistributing income as it used to.

Those who have direct or indirect access to the wealth generated by the new continental order will do all right. Incomes will grow for corporate and state managers, professionals, the small core of highly skilled technicians. More and more their income and consumption patterns and their lifestyles will resemble those of their counterparts in the United States and Mexico. Less and less will they resemble those of other groups in Canadian society.

As the divide grows, the values of equity and justice that bind us as a community and a nation weaken. Increasingly, rich and poor, first world and third world, North and South cease to distinguish nations, but rather regions and social groups according to their position in the hierarchy in the new continental order.

The transnational corporate community saw the Canadian-U.S. agreement as a crucial stepping-stone to a continental free-trade zone. Secure access to a low-wage area and to long-term energy supplies was essential to their global restructuring plans.

The free-trade agreement incorporates the *maquiladora* in the new continental economy in an informal way. It is clearly speeding up the restructuring of the Canadian economy, intensifying the downward pull on social and environmental standards, and accelerating the loss of jobs and production. However the corporations want to entrench the relationship in a formal three-nation treaty. A future Canadian government could, under the present arrangement, put up barriers to goods coming from Mexico on the grounds that the extreme exploitation of labour and degradation of the environment are forms of unfair trade. A future American government could do the same or scrap the *maquiladora* program entirely. A formal treaty would not only prevent such actions but also broaden and deepen the relationship by extending the *maquiladora* concept to all of Mexico.

From a Canadian corporate perspective, there is a certain urgency: the Conservative government is extremely unpopular, and no future government would be as committed to the corporate agenda. It is therefore important to move quickly before the next election. Moreover, opposition to free trade is very high in Canada. A large majority of the population see it as hurting the country and certainly don't want it extended to Mexico. Therefore, the next Canadian government might be unwilling to proceed with trilateral free trade and might consider scrapping the original agreement.

In the spring of 1990, the BCNI hired former trade negotiator Michael Hart to do a study of how the free-trade deal could be expanded to include Mexico. Hart confirmed the importance of a continental accord "to further lock in the market orientation" of the transformed Canadian economy. Hart also said that the price of a deal for Canada would likely be new concessions under a re-opened FTA.

The main reason we have to be at the bargaining table with the United States and Mexico, according to government and business, is "to protect our hard-won gains" in the Canada-U.S. round. They are vague on what those gains might have been. They continue to say, despite the carnage, that it's too early to tell what effect the trade deal has had on Canada.

Hollow is the argument that we have to be at the table to protect unidentifiable gains for which we paid an extortionate price. No doubt we will pay once again to protect that illusory market access, in the Mexican round. And we will pay again and again as the United States swallows up the entire hemisphere.

The United States has told Canada quite clearly that we will have to pay again. Trade representative Carla Hills says the FTA "sets the floor," from which they want further concessions. The free-trade deal is open for re-negotiation, although the Conservative government isn't sure whether to admit this publicly. Ministers and officials regularly contradict each other on the subject.

Everything is on the table — the few things, that is, they did not get in the first round: culture, intellectual property, and agriculture. The so-called cultural exemption in the FTA lets us keep the existing protections of a very small portion of our own market and stops us from carving out a bigger share. Now the Americans want to get rid of Canadian-content requirements, Telefilm Canada, the Canada Council, foreign-ownership restrictions, special tax deductions, etc. As the Mexicans have no objections to culture being on the table, the United States will play us off against the Mexicans in this negotiation. There is no obligation to reach an agreement in which all rules are the same for all parties.

As for intellectual property, the price will be extensive protection to U.S. corporate property, such as patents and trademarks. In the first round, we greatly watered down our drug-patent laws to give the giant pharmaceutical companies more protection; but we didn't do away with "compulsory licensing," which requires that, after a certain amount of time, the companies have to allow other companies to manufacture their products. In exchange for a handsome royalty, they lose their monopoly. The resulting competition lowers drug prices to the consumer, but it also lowers corporate profits.

The watering-down of the drug laws in the free-trade agreement has already increased prices dramatically. Jack Kay, of the Canadian Drug Manufacturers' Association, says that the price of new products has jumped from $1 to $3 per tablet. Further changes can only make the situation worse.

Mexico has just passed a new patent law that is identical to the U.S. law, exactly what the U.S. drug manufacturers want. The Americans dearly want to entrench these laws in an intellectual-property code in a continental trade deal. Canada will be under intense pressure to adopt the U.S.-Mexican standard. If Canada resists, it may, for example, be given less favourable access to U.S. government contracts.

The Canadian government has put some of its own demands on the table: increased protection for Canadian investors in the United States and increased access to American government procurement. Once again the Conservatives are prepared to trade away our culture for a few government contracts.

The Canadian corporate sector wants a continental trade deal that will give them the same secure access to cheap Mexican labour as U.S. corporations have, as they do not want the Americans to have a competitive edge. They want to be able to locate freely in Mexico, import materials from Canada or the United States freely, and export anywhere on the continent without restriction or fear of restriction.

As well, they want to make sure they do not lose U.S. market share to Mexico. The United States is the largest market for both Canada and Mexico; it accounts for roughly three-quarters of their trade. (Canada supplies 25 percent of U.S. imports of auto engines; Mexico supplies 13 percent. Canada produces 9 percent of U.S. electric-power equipment imports; Mexico produces 19 percent.) Canadian business wants to ensure that Mexican-based companies don't end up with more advantageous rules on tariffs, quotas, or subsidies; or rules governing investment or the settlement of disputes; or access to U.S. government contracts, etc.

Canada-Mexico trade appears to be small, just over $2 billion annually. Mexico, according to Statistics Canada, exports to Canada three times as much as it imports. However, the imbalance is at least another five times greater because much *maquiladora* production enters the United States already stamped "Made in USA" or quickly becomes absorbed in American final products that eventually find their way into Canada.

It should be remembered that about three-quarters of the trade among the three nations, excluding resources, is the movement of products within different facilities of the same transnational corporations. It is very important that we understand the implications of this: in an unregulated continental market the corporations decide what gets produced, where, and by whom. Governments in all three countries, at all levels, end up competing to offer the most attractive (i.e., the highest) incentives, the most favourable climate; workers end up competing to offer the most attractive (i.e., the lowest) wages and benefits.

Mexico: Land of Opportunity

Specific segments of Corporate Canada have particular interests in wanting Canada to be part of a trilateral trade deal. Canadian banks, led by the Royal Bank and the Bank of Montreal, hold $5 billion of Mexico's foreign debt. They receive more in interest payments every year than the value of all Canadian exports to Mexico. They see a trade deal as the way to ensure that oil and *maquiladora* exports will increase. This new wealth is their best guarantee that Mexico will remain able to service its bank loans. (It should be noted that the Canadian banks continue to collect huge interest payments on their Mexican loans even though they have written off half of these loans as unpayable. The write-off was eased by generous tax subsidies from the Conservative government. A Commons External Affairs Committee report estimates that subsidized bank write-offs of third-world debt have cost the Treasury $3 billion.)

The banks have other interests as well. Mexico is about to reprivatize its banking system and has earmarked a third of it for foreign investors. The Canadian banks believe they would have a better crack at a piece of this action inside a free-trade agreement. They would also stand to benefit from new opportunities that would open up for

Canadian corporations as Mexico speeds up the sale of state enterprises and allocates major contracts to foreigners. Companies such as Bell Canada, Northern Telecom, and Spar are angling for opportunities in telecommunications; Bombardier in urban transit equipment; Noranda in mining, and so forth. Free trade, they all believe, will give them an inside track.

Although Mexico is a poor country, it has a narrow stratum of very rich people. This translates into a wealthy market that Canadian business has not yet entered very aggressively. The richest 10 percent of the Mexican population, about 8.5 million consumers, have more than twice as big a share of the national income as the richest 10 percent of Canadians. As Dale Scott, vice-president of Bell Canada, said, "We are learning fast that Mexicans like conspicuous consumption and want the sexiest $1,400 phones."

The Salinas government strategy for free-trade–driven economic recovery is very much directed at dynamizing this small, high-income segment of the economy. He is betting that free trade will create a psychology of stability that will cause an inflow of wealth, both foreign capital and some of the estimated $100 billion rich Mexicans hold outside the country. A return of capital to Mexico with free trade — Peat Marwick estimates that the inflow could be as high as $25 billion — would translate into a big demand for imports. Canadian corporations want a share.

The Salinas economic strategy, as Professor Adolpho Aguilar Zinser of the National University of Mexico points out, is also constructed to further dislocate, impoverish, and exclude the majority of Mexicans. Carlos Heridia, who works with the development organization Equipo Pueblo, says that a "free trade agreement would improve the conditions of probably 10 percent of the population — the major exporters, the financial sector, and the elite of business and politics. On the other hand it would deepen the social inequality that we have in this country."

One in five Mexicans is now officially unemployed. A much larger group are the underemployed, the *marginales*. They work at numerous part-time or temporary jobs, eking out a bare subsistence at the edges of the Mexican economy. Their incomes, like those of the *maquiladora* workers, are kept extremely low by deliberate government strategy.

Forty million Mexicans are farmers. Most work on communal lands called *ejidos*. Both Mexican and U.S. corporate interests are converting more and more *ejido* land to agribusiness operations producing export crops, and opening up Mexican agriculture to American imports. Mexico now produces one-quarter of the fruits and vegetables consumed in the United States. Mexico also imports one-half of its basic foodstuffs: corn, wheat, beans, and milk. Ten years ago Mexico was a self-sufficient food producer.

This situation has caused major disruption in the rural communities. Federico Ovalle, of the Independent Coalition of Campesino Organisations, explains: "The government opened our borders to U.S. soybeans and rice at half the price of Mexican grains. Farmers are now having to sell far below production costs, if they can sell at all. This is just the beginning of what we are going to see under free trade."

Despite the false promises and failed predictions of the first round, the Canadian political and corporate merchants of deceit are shamelessly preaching the illusory virtues of extending free trade to Mexico. Even some critics are saying that we have no choice now, that it is inevitable.

Perhaps the most distasteful argument being used to sell free trade with Mexico is that it will raise the living standards of ordinary Mexicans. The C.D. Howe Institute called it a "way of alleviating poverty of the masses." Alf Powis, head of the giant Noranda Inc., says simply, "If you want to help them, give them free trade." Critics of the free-trade model, including those in the development community, such as CUSO and OXFAM, are being portrayed as blocking the interests of the Mexican people, as if unfettered corporate greed produces development and justice. This is the ultimate expression of what the Bishop of Victoria, Remi DeRoo, calls "the serious moral disorder" that is continental free trade.

Mexican labour economist Alejandro Alvarez describes free trade as the "maquilization of Mexico." He stresses that "the *maquiladora* is not a project of national development. Its effects are truly devastating for our most precious resource, our work-force." He warns that the supposed comparative advantage of miserable wages "could precipitate political and social conflicts of great intensity."

The effect of free trade is best put by Raul Escobar, leader of one of the few independent unions in Mexico, the Ford workers' union. "We are already living with free trade, although there has not been a formal treaty with that name. What it means is that companies have the freedom to have plants in Mexico without real unions, without paying decent wages or fair taxes, and without protecting our health and safety or the environment. The Mexican workers have the freedom to work for almost nothing.

"And workers in the United States [and Canada] have the freedom to lose their jobs."

3.

THE BETRAYAL OF SOCIETY

"I've heard the anguish of people who have lost their jobs."

THESE WERE THE WORDS OF FINANCE MINIS-
ter Michael Wilson as he presented his 1991 budget to a
nation buried deep in winter recession. It was a mean
budget for hard times, a callous response to a human crisis,
that cut vulnerable people loose when their need was
greatest. Like its predecessors, Wilson's budget is part of a
systematic effort to tear down our social programs; to shift
wealth to the rich at the expense of the majority; and to
create conditions that will make unemployment, poverty,
and insecurity a permanent reality for a large and growing
sector of our population.

It is ironic that the Conservatives came to power in
1984, the year in which George Orwell set his futuristic
novel of political manipulation. The story of the Conservatives' remaking of Canadian society in the meaner, crueller image of its southern neighbour is told in classic
Orwellian doublespeak. Social programs to be cut are a

"sacred trust." "Fewer taxes" means more taxes. "Fair taxes" means unfair taxes. "Better public services" means worse public services. "More jobs" means fewer jobs.

When Michael Wilson said in his 1986 budget speech that he wanted to "spread the tax burden more equitably," he meant that he was going to lower taxes for the rich. When he said in 1987 that he wanted "to improve our social programs and provide more help for those in need," he meant that he was going to remove the structures that buttress our most vulnerable citizens against economic uncertainty. When he promised in the 1990 budget "a consistent and comprehensive plan to ensure Canadians can benefit from a rising standard of living and a quality of life second to none in the world," he meant he was creating a society in which compassion is replaced by survival of the fittest, in which the ties of community are replaced by the law of the jungle, and in which winners are few and losers are many.

Almost three years into the promised new dawn of free-trade prosperity, half a million jobs have vanished, according to official figures. Half of the 435,000 jobs lost in the manufacturing sector are gone for good. Officially there are now a million and a half people out of work across the country — more than 10 percent of the work-force — and the numbers are growing. Not included in these figures are the 800,000 people who have given up looking for work or who are doing part-time or temporary jobs because they can't find full-time jobs. One in six of the country's working population is unemployed or underemployed.

Health and Welfare Canada reports that, for the first time in our history, more than two million Canadians and their dependants, 10 percent of the population, depend on social assistance or welfare payments; and their ranks are growing. The number of homeless — 200,000 at last count — is also growing quickly. The Canadian Association of Food Banks reports that 600,000 people need food banks to survive; one-third are children. (In Toronto there are three food banks for every McDonald's restaurant.)

Yet even these shocking national unemployment statistics don't reveal the full picture in different regions and communities. Atlantic Canada never recovered from the 1982 recession; it didn't participate in the so-called great economic boom of the 1980s. Demand for its primary resources remained weak and prices stayed low. Corporations took their profits without re-investing in the region. In many communities unemployment never fell below 15 percent. The Atlantic economy, highly dependent on public-sector involvement, has been strangled by Conservative policies. It has lost rail, air, and postal services. It has lost military bases and public television stations. The federal government has slashed social and education spending. It cut back regional-development assistance and shifted the goal of fishery regulation from sustaining communities to supporting the large corporations.

Hundreds of communities in northern and outlying regions across the country are facing the same grim reality. As fish plants, pulp mills, steel mills, and smelters are mothballed, people are fighting a losing battle to remain in their communities. Families are splitting up under the pressure of members leaving in search of work, and communities die as entire families move away.

In the industrial heartland of Ontario and Quebec, the crisis in manufacturing has been the worst since the Depression of the 1930s. Companies are closing down and moving production south of the border. Business and personal bankruptcies are at their highest levels in Canadian history. People are losing their jobs; if they are lucky enough to find other work, it is more often than not at lower pay, less skilled, and temporary or part-time. Statistics Canada reported that, during the 1982 recession, one-half of the workers who lost their jobs but managed to find new work lost, on average, one-third of their previous income level. The indications are that it is worse this time around. Skilled tradespeople, most of whom have never been unemployed, are facing the prospect of UI and then welfare. Older or immigrant workers who lack language or other basic educational skills, and who face prejudice from employers, may never work again. "That's what Mulroney means by restructuring the economy," says Janet Dassinger, skills-training co-ordinator at the Toronto Labour Education Centre, "slamming the door in the faces of the women and men who thought they could build a future by the honest work of their hands."

Farm communities across the country are at the breaking-point. Ten years of depressed prices and heavy debt loads have forced one Canadian farmer in eight off his or her land. One in five is technically bankrupt, on financial life-support, according to the Commons Agriculture Committee. The family farm faces extinction, squeezed by Conservative policies that favour big agribusiness corporations.

Hundreds of thousands of Canadians are crowding into urban centres in search of work, intensifying already acute social pressures. Official unemployment is 13 percent in Montreal, 9 percent in Toronto, and 10 percent in Vancouver. Affordable housing is practically non-existent. Welfare caseloads have skyrocketed. The system is cracking under the weight.

People are angry at being uprooted; often this anger is misdirected, resulting in family, ethnic, or racial violence. Or it is unfocused, anxiety mixed with confusion and resignation, a feeling that one must merely adjust to "forces out there" over which individuals have no control.

People tend to blame themselves: if I can't find a job, it is my fault. If I get retrained and still can't find a job, it is still my fault. And if I'm working at two jobs that together don't pay as much as my old job so we can keep our house, and I don't have time for retraining, that, too, is my fault.

The 1980s saw the rich get richer at the expense of the rest of us — the reverse of a trend of narrowing somewhat the gap between income groups. The top 20 percent of Canadian income-holders increased their share of the national income pie from 39.9 to 41.9 percent. Although it seems modest, it represents an extra $10 billion taken from the rest us. To find a comparable shift in income distribution you have to go back to the 1920s.

Real wages of workers, that is, income after inflation, grew more slowly during the 1980s than in any decade in the twentieth century, far below the growth in productivity, that is, output of goods or services per hour of work. The federal minimum wage of $4 per hour is lower than every province's legal minimum. The Conservatives haven't raised it since 1986. Just to regain the purchasing power that it has lost since 1975 it would have to rise to $7.50.

Michael Wilson lamented in 1985 that Canada did not have enough rich people; but he has done a good job of changing the situation. Canada has some very rich people. *Forbes* magazine puts three Canadian families — the Reichmanns, the Thomsons, and the Irvings — among the twenty richest on earth. Increases in salaries of corporate executives have outpaced their workers' wages throughout the 1980s, by 25 percent. The average salaries of the CEOs of major corporations was fifty times that of their lowest-paid employee; this is second only to the

United States, where the gap is eighty-five times. (To compare, the gap in Japan is only seventeen times.) A study by Hay Management Consultants Ltd. says that free-trade–driven integration "will increase the pressure to equalize compensation at the executive level," that is, move salaries upward to U.S. levels.

Betraying a Trust

A nation's economy is supposed to meet the individual and collective needs of its citizens, to reflect their priorities and values. It is not an end in itself, but a tool of national development, a means to achieving the desired ends of the society. Ultimately we have to judge the performance of an economy in terms of those ends.

Canadians believe deeply that each citizen has certain entitlements or rights: to health care, education, old-age security, unemployment insurance, etc., and that these rights should be financed and administered largely by the public sector. These entitlements express the community values that emerged from the deep trauma of the 1930s and matured into the social consensus by which we define ourselves as a nation. As the Spicer Commission heard, most Canadians are still committed to these beliefs.

The Conservative government has ignored that consensus and has shredded these programs that are part of our national identity. It has truly betrayed a sacred trust and has done so deviously, without public understanding or consent.

Related to this sense of entitlement is a belief that income should be distributed more fairly. A major role of government is to redistribute income within our society. Seven years of Conservative government have seen inequality grow faster than at any time since the 1920s. The rich have gotten richer; the rest of us poorer. The tax system, already tilted in favour of the wealthy, has become increasingly unbalanced. The growing number of millionaires and billionaires balances the swelling ranks of the poor and destitute. Wage increases have lagged behind inflation, behind productivity gains, and far, far behind executive salary increases. Poor regions of the country have become poorer as government transfers shrink. Federal cutbacks for regional development violate constitutional commitments.

In violating the principles of tax fairness, the Conservative government has accentuated a trend begun by the previous Liberal government and helped to bring on a financial crisis. The enormous debt that this government has imposed upon us is not the result of runaway spending on social and other programs, as they would have us believe; but rather the culmination of years of tax subsidies to large corporations and the rich, and snowballing debt charges incurred to cover the resulting revenue shortfall. In fact, the government has used the debt to veil a massive cutback in program spending. In doing so, they have discredited all government in the eyes of many Canadians and greatly constrained the ability to provide the public goods and services that Canadians expect.

Canadians, as public-opinion polls consistently confirm, attach the highest priority to full employment, to an economy that provides decent jobs for those who are able and willing to work. The Liberals began to renege on this commitment in the mid-1970s, but the Conservatives have rejected the commitment altogether. They openly embrace the orthodox economic wisdom that unemployment must not be allowed to fall much below 8 percent, lest a secure work-force become an unco-operative work-force. The Conservatives have institutionalized mass unemployment even during periods of rapid economic growth. Indeed, not since the 1930s has a Canadian government been so willing to sacrifice millions of Canadians to unemployment in the name of "protecting the dollar" and "fiscal responsibility." The Conservatives pay lipservice to the goal of full employment, but history provides no example of a government that has achieved full employment using an anti-inflation policy. For the Conservatives to even imply that full employment lies at the end of this road is dishonest. For them to say we have to wait a decade, as their last budget forecast indicates, is immoral.

Most Canadians are aware that our planet is an extremely fragile ecosystem. They realize that economic growth has polluted our air and water, contaminated our soil, stripped our forests, killed our wildlife, and depleted our resources. Most accept that preserving the environment must be central to all decisions we make on the economy.

The Conservative government mouths platitudes about the environment, but economic priorities such as an energy mega-project or a water-diversion scheme always push aside environmental considerations. Unbridled, corporations force down environmental standards just as they force down wages. Legislators who seek to strengthen environmental standards must always confront the threat by mobile corporations to pack up and move to more "sympathetic" jurisdictions. Free or deregulated trade is deeply contrary to protecting the environment. Letting the market dictate how resources are utilized throws conservation out the window.

Canadians have long supported the mixed economy implied by "peace, order, and good government." We realize that our survival as a nation requires a strong role for government as a regulator of economic activity and as a direct participant in the economy. Peculiarities of geography, population, and climate have given rise to many crown corporations. In some cases they were created to provide vital goods and services where the market failed. In others they were created specifically to exclude the market from a given activity; a national airline, a national railway, a national postal service, a national broadcasting corporation, a national grain-marketing agency, a national oil company, provincial electrical utilities, companies that hold strategic biotech or aerospace technologies, and many more. For the most part they have established solid reputations for efficiency and quality. Canadians have historically supported crown corporations, not only as vital instruments of national economic development, but as symbols. Some, such as the CBC and CN, have, as Canadians told the Spicer Commission, acquired the "power of our shared mythology."

The Conservatives have sold off two dozen of these public corporations, which employ about 100,000 Canadians: Air Canada, Petro-Canada, de Havilland, Connaught BioSciences. (Many other public services have been privatized through "contracting out," the transfer of individual government programs and functions to the private sector.) Some have been sold at fire-sale prices. Others have fallen into the hands of foreign corporations. Still others have been dispersed through public share issues, ending up in the hands of a small group of wealthy Canadians.

Some of these privatized corporations have gone bankrupt. Many have cut back their work-forces and diminished the quality of service. Conservatives have tried to discredit corporations still awaiting the auction block by strangling their funding and removing their public mandate. The Tory dismantling of public enterprise has been wholesale and indiscriminate: Tory ideology dictates that all public corporations must go. Therefore there has been no objective assessment of whether selling off this enterprise or dumping that service is good for the country.

Canadians believe that, in order to assure our economic health and our ability to develop as a nation, we need to own our businesses. We have tolerated a high degree of foreign (mainly American) ownership, the highest in the industrial world. Most of us believe that we have gone far enough; many believe foreign ownership should be reduced. The Conservatives' open-door investment policy has reversed a fifteen-year effort to take back some of our economy. Tory interest-rate policies have also prompted governments and large corporations to borrow, not at home, but on the less expensive international money markets. As a result, Canada has become the world's second-largest foreign debtor. Not only have these policies led to an enormous drain of wealth through interest and dividend payments, but they have also constrained our ability to pursue development policies in accordance with our own priorities.

Universal Medical Care
Medicare is the most cherished of our social programs. It is funded partly through financial transfers from the federal government to the provinces. In 1984, these transfer payments covered roughly one-half of the program's cost. The other half came from the provinces, which are responsible for the administration of the program.

The Conservatives began their sabotage of Medicare in their very first budget, in 1985.

First they undercut the formula by which transfer payments were made. Transfers used to be paid in line with the growth of the economy measured by GNP. If the economy grew by 6 percent, then transfer payments would grow by 6 percent. The Tories reduced the growth in transfer payments to two percentage points below that of the economy (GNP minus 2). The shortfall would have to be made up by the provinces.

Federal transfer payments to the provinces are made up of two parts: one part is a lump sum of cash and the other is based on the calculated value of tax points transferred to the provinces under a federal-provincial arrangement set up back in 1977. At that time, the federal government gave over to the provinces a certain amount of its taxing power. The idea was that the provinces would then direct the revenue from this additional taxing power to Medicare, over and above the half-share they were paying already. Even though the provinces were now doing the tax collecting, the fiction was maintained that this additional income was still part of the federal transfer payment.

The calculated value of the tax-points portion of the transfer grows automatically at the same rate as the economy, if federal taxes remain constant. However, their value has been growing faster than the economy because the government has been raising taxes.

Consider the following example. Assume for simplicity that, at the end of a given year, half the federal transfer was tax points and half was cash. Say tax points grow this year at 8 percent and the economy grows at 6 percent. Under the old formula the actual increase in the federal cash transfer would have been 4 percent. With the Tory cut in the transfer to 4 percent (GNP minus 2), the actual increase in cash that the federal government has to hand over at this year's end is zero: the tax-point increase fulfils the full obligation of the federal transfer.

The Conservative government reduced the transfer-payments formula a second time in its 1990 budget; it now stands at three percentage points less than the growth in GNP. Worse still, it has frozen transfer payments to 1994. Because the tax-points portion continues to grow, the only way the government can freeze transfer payments is by cutting the cash it transfers. The cuts have been huge. Between 1990–91 and 1991–92, federal cash transfers for health care are dropping from $7.2 billion to $6.1 billion, according to the latest estimates from Health and Welfare Canada.

There are two consequences. First, the cumulative effect of this systematic gouging will have drained an estimated $22 billion from the health system between 1985 and 1994. If the Tories are still in power by 1998, the total withdrawal over thirteen years will be an estimated $46 billion. (This is from a prime minister who, when asked during the free-trade election to guarantee that he would not slash social programs, responded that "to answer questions like that would be to dignify them. We have no intention of doing anything of the kind.")

The other consequence is even more ominous. At the present rate of decline, federal cash transfers to most provinces will be zero by around 1997–98. With no federal money going to Medicare, the federal government will no longer have a lever to enforce national standards as enshrined in the Canada Health Act: universality, accessibility, comprehensiveness of service, portability, and public administration. Universal Medicare will be automatically replaced by eleven highly uneven provincial/territorial systems. Federal health minister Benoît Bouchard says he is "ready to put everything on the table. ... If is it decided to give health services totally and exclusively to the provinces, I can live with that."

The process has already begun. The Quebec government has introduced a $5 hospital user fee and intends to allow extra billing by doctors; both are in violation of Medicare. The Manitoba finance minister, Clayton Manness, has stated that his government is sympathetic to replacing Medicare with a provincial program. With federal funding disappearing, he argues, "we cannot attain the standards." The British Columbia government also wants to take over full control of health care. A finance department discussion paper says that national standards get in the way of provincial efforts to "control program costs." Alberta wants to bring in a two-tier system: one for basic services funded by government and another for undefined services funded by private insurance. Seniors with incomes greater than $5,500 now have to pay one-quarter of the cost of items such as walkers, canes, and home oxygen tanks. The death-knell of Medicare has been sounded.

Moreover, federal cutbacks are hitting hardest in the poorest provinces. Newfoundland spent twice as much, relative to GDP, as Alberta to maintain a similar level of health care even before the Tories started to slash. It has now begun to cut back hospital beds and health-care staff. Extra billing and user fees are not far behind.

The Conservative government's planned withdrawal from Medicare by the end of the decade is not a coincidence. It corresponds to the seven-year deadline to reach a common subsidies code under the free-trade agreement. The Americans have long viewed Medicare as an unfair subsidy and raised it during the original negotiations. It would undoubtedly be on the table during the subsidies round, so what better way to avoid the embarrassment of being seen to be caving in than by dismantling the system before the issue comes to the table.

The corporate community has been pushing extra hard lately for the dismembering of Medicare and other social programs. Why? "We can't afford them, in these times of restraint," they usually say. "We have to target our scarce resources to those most in need." "Targeting" is a code-word for cutback. Targeted programs are poor programs.

It is useful to recall what the BCNI said during the 1988 election campaign in *Straight Talk on Free Trade*, the advertising supplement that blanketed the media. It asked, "What about our social programs like pensions and medi-care?" It answered: "They are not threatened in any way by the Free Trade Agreement." "Won't Canadian business lobby to reduce spending on social and other pro-grams?" it asked. "Not at all," it answered. Now the BCNI strongly supports the government's cuts to health-care transfers to the provinces, arguing that generous social programs are threatening our standard of living.

Edmond King, CEO of Wood Gundy, believes that the provinces should implement "fees . . . that would main-tain universality but shift some of the burden to users of the health-care system." This is doublespeak. User fees are incompatible with universality. Raymond Cyr, CEO of Bell Canada Enterprises Inc. and member of the BCNI, told an audience at the Canadian Club of Montreal that "the federal government should be more concerned about global competitiveness of Canadian industry than about questions such as user fees for health services. . . . You can be a Canadian without necessarily being attached to uni-versal national standards in services. . . . It is a mistake to argue about the notion of universality and use it almost as a synonym for being a Canadian."

The Tories are killing Medicare by stealth so Canadians can't see what is going on. The strategy is to pay lip-service to the concept but remove its supports: dry up its funding gradually and surreptitiously. Remove its enforcement mechanisms. Strangle it slowly and deny that you're doing it. When people realize, too late, that it is gone, blame the provinces. Monique Bégin, former minister of health in the Trudeau government, warned during the free-trade debate that "Medicare is a fragile institution vulnerable . . . to slow, quiet, behind-the-scenes erosion." The Tories have exploited that vulnerability with the same cunning they have used to bring in free trade and so many of their other policies.

Family Allowances and Pensions

More devious even than its attack on health transfers to the provinces has been the Mulroney government's gutting and ultimate destruction of the universality of two important social programs — family allowances and old-age pensions. They have done this through an ingenious device known as the "tax clawback."

Michael Wilson tried to cut back these programs in his first budget in 1985 by limiting payment increases to three points less than inflation. (For example, if inflation rose by 5 percent, the payments would go up only 2 percent.) The huge public outcry against the proposed pension cutbacks took the new government by surprise. It retreated and restored full indexation, although it maintained its partial deindexing of family-allowance payments and other child-benefit tax exemptions.

Four years after the 1985 fiasco, the government decided to take another run at pensions and family allowances. It came in the 1989 budget, only four months after Brian Mulroney had made a campaign promise to a group of seniors in P.E.I. "As long as I am prime minister, social benefits, particularly benefits for the elderly, will be improved, not diminished by this government." In

Quebec City he said, "Never would I sign an accord that would have the effect of threatening my own mother's pension."

Here's how the clawback diminishes Mrs. Mulroney's pension. Seniors who have incomes of $50,000 begin to lose their pensions to taxes. As their income goes up, the tax rate increases. Seniors with incomes of $65,000 will lose half of their old-age pensions and those with incomes of $76,000 see their pensions completely taxed back.

It appears that only a small group of well-off Canadians are affected, but there is a catch. The government has partially delinked the thresholds from inflation. The income level at which the tax begins will rise at three percentage points less than the rate of inflation. Thus, the $50,000 threshold will fall to $40,000 after only eight years. After thirty years it will fall to $20,000.

Thus, a twenty-five-year-old worker who today earns $28,000, an average industrial wage, whose income grows at the same rate as the rate of inflation, will see little or no pension when she or he retires in forty years.

The clawback gouges family allowances more rapidly. It begins at a single income of $50,000, close to the average family income in Canada. The taxback rate increases so fast that someone earning $56,500 and supporting two children will not keep a penny of family allowance. Moreover, as with pensions, income thresholds will decrease so that in a short time even low-income families will be affected.

The death of family allowance means that Canadian families no longer have, as right of citizenship, government recognition of the value of raising children. Granted the amount of the payment is small — for some it is just symbolic — but for many families it is an essential part of the family budget.

The corporate argument for taxing back universal family allowances was that they should only go to those who need it. "Why," it asked, "should a bank president earning $500,000 a year get the family allowance?" This clever piece of rhetoric side-stepped the important question, which is not how the $400 family allowance should be taxed but rather how the other $499,600 of the president's income should be taxed.

The scandal is that the bank president's salary is taxed at the same rate as that of a schoolteacher. The Conservatives lowered the highest federal income-tax bracket from an already shamefully low 34 percent to 29 percent in 1987. Restoring the old rate would raise an additional $2 billion in revenues, four times the government savings from the clawback. (Obviously, what we need is a more progressive income-tax structure to ensure that high-income earners pay a fairer share of taxes. This would guarantee enough revenue to maintain and improve our social programs.)

So, why the corporate Conservative assault on universality? The argument that we can no longer afford universal programs so we must provide them only to those most in need is seductive. However, this so-called targeting of programs inevitably means weakening them. If a program benefits all of us, we have a vested interest in ensuring that quality is maintained. A program targeted to the poor becomes a poor program because the rest of us don't have a stake in maintaining its quality, and the poor don't have enough political clout to ensure that they are well served.

Targeted programs divide the rich from the poor, and from the somewhat poor. Universal social programs encourage a sense of solidarity, of community within our society. They are basic human rights, part of who we are as Canadians.

Universality is part of what distinguishes Canada from

the United States. Their social programs are not a right of citizenship: people have to prove they are poor enough to qualify, and the need keeps getting redefined downward. The U.S. Medicaid program, a targeted program for the poor, is far inferior to our Medicare. There are thirty-seven million people in the United States who cannot afford private insurance but are not sufficiently poor to qualify for Medicaid. These people have no access to any form of health insurance. As U.S. Medicaid shows us, once the principle of universality is broken, it becomes easier for a government to take responsibility for fewer and fewer of its citizens.

The corporations also want to destroy universality in order to force our social-support system in line with the inferior U.S. system. It is not because a weaker system is cheaper. For example, the Canadian health-care system is far less costly than the U.S. system, but private health care is big business. There are profits to be made. Moreover, a weak social safety net breeds insecurity. Insecure workers are less likely to protest bad wages and bad working conditions, or leave a bad job.

In the prevailing corporate vision of competitiveness a compliant, docile work-force is an absolute necessity. The C.D. Howe Institute wrote in its 1989 budget brief that Canada's existing social net has been "destructive of work incentives, an obstacle to needed economic adjustment." In the name of competitiveness and the free-trade level playing field, the Mulroney government is tearing away those very social programs that embody the values that define who we are.

Jobs, Jobs, Jobs
The highest measure of a nation's commitment to economic justice is the extent to which it provides decent jobs

for all its citizens who are able and willing to work. Commitment to full employment enhances a society's output and ensures a fairer distribution of a society's wealth.

In the two decades after the Second World War, Canadian governments were genuinely committed to full employment. Never during that period did the unemployment rate rise above 5 percent. To have done so would have brought a national outcry sufficient to bring down a government. After the mid-1970s, unemployment rates rose in Canada, soaring to 13 percent nationally during the 1982 recession. Thereafter, despite five years of rapid economic expansion, unemployment never fell much below 7 percent.

An unfortunate consequence of prolonged high unemployment is that familiarity breeds a widespread sense of resignation, a feeling that unemployment is somehow an anonymous and inevitable evil.

After the mid-1970s the pattern of unemployment in industrialized countries began to change. In some countries mass unemployment has appeared and has stayed. In others it has remained low. Why? The main cause of this difference has been the relative commitment of governments. For example, both Sweden, under a social-democratic government, and Japan, under a conservative government, have managed to maintain unemployment levels well below 5 percent, even during recessions. Both governments consider full employment to be a top priority; both have strong institutions to back up this commitment. Neither cuts spending nor keeps interest rates high in time of recession. They both have active labour-market policies, such as training and subsidized employment, to ensure that the supply and demand for labour stays in balance. Finally, they do not use high unemployment as a means to achieve other policy goals, such as low inflation.

This last point is particularly important when compared with Canadian government policies. The Mulroney government has always given first importance to fighting inflation. It deliberately keeps unemployment high in order to get inflation down. Only at some ill-defined, indefinitely postponed time does it predict unemployment will fall. No industrialized country has achieved full employment in this way.

The Conservative position is reflected in that of the Bank of Canada. The Bank holds that an unemployment rate below 8 percent causes inflation to rise. Accordingly, it uses high interest rates to depress economic activity and prevent unemployment from falling. Former finance minister Michael Wilson's 1991 budget set inflation targets but not targets to lower unemployment. On the contrary, his own economic forecasts clearly state that a consequence of his policies will be near double-digit unemployment for at least the next five years.

Canada developed its unemployment-insurance system during the Second World War. The program is based on several principles: that economic development was uneven across Canada; that some regions of the country had chronically higher rates of unemployment than others; and that government had direct responsibility for unemployment and would provide income support adequate to enable workers to remain in their communities or regions until new jobs became available.

Workers, employers, and government contributed to the program. Government provided extra benefits in regions where unemployment rose above 4 percent. Fishermen in Atlantic Canada were granted special benefits because of the seasonal nature of their work. UI, as it is called, became one of the basic tenets of the Canadian social contract and has served us well. During the 1982 recession, for example, almost one-third of Canadians were beneficiaries of this program.

The Tories and the corporations are opposed to the concept of UI because it gives too much power to workers. It gives them protection in case of being fired, and the confidence to quit a bad job to search for a better one. Free trade required that UI be harmonized downward to the U.S. system to avoid the competitive disadvantage of Canadian employees having greater bargaining power in the job market. The former head of the Canadian Manufacturers' Association, Laurent Thibault, testifying before a parliamentary committee in 1980, forecast accurately what would happen under free trade: "As we ask our industries to compete toe-to-toe with American industries . . . we are forced to create the same conditions in Canada that exist in the United States, whether it is unemployment insurance schemes, workers' compensation, the cost of government, the level of taxation or whatever."

The government held off the radical surgery until free trade was safely passed. Five months after the election, it withdrew all government contributions ($3 billion in 1989), including the special fishermen's benefit. Canada is now the only industrialized country, other than the United States, where government does not contribute to unemployment insurance. By privatizing UI, the Tories absolved themselves of all responsibility for employment.

The changes hit low-income workers the hardest. As a rule their jobs are least secure, and they change jobs more often. The Tories lengthened the UI qualifying period and shortened the benefit period — for example, in Halifax, Moncton, Regina, and Vancouver, workers now need an extra six weeks' work to qualify. Thus, the Tories have

dumped hundreds of thousands of unemployed onto the
welfare rolls of municipalities and provinces.

UI used to be comprehensive, covering four of five
unemployed workers. The Tories' changes move it closer
to the lean and mean U.S. system, in which fewer than one
in three workers qualifies and those who do get less money
for a shorter time.

Amercian interests didn't like our UI program and
wanted it changed. At the upcoming negotiations on common rules for subsidies, part of the unfinished free-trade
agenda, the Tories can inform their U.S. masters that, by
the time the seven-year deadline arrives, all our social and
regional-development principles that the United States
finds objectionable will have been destroyed.

Tax Subsidies for the Rich

Our tax system has never reflected our fundamental values
of fairness and equity. However, since the Conservatives
came to power in 1984, the tax system has strayed much
farther from that goal. Michael Wilson, in his eight years
as finance minister, was a Robin Hood for the rich. Osgoode Hall law professor Neil Brook calls our system "a
disgrace to one of the most affluent countries in the
world." The gap between values and reality is intolerable.

The National Council on Welfare calculated that by
1988 the tax bill for the working poor had increased 44
percent, while that of the wealthiest Canadians decreased
by 6 percent. A study for the Institute for Research on
Public Policy found that the average tax bill for the top 1
percent (those with incomes greater than $114,000) fell an
average of $1,500 each year from 1984 to 1989. While
corporate profits soared in the 1980s, corporate tax payments fell sharply, thanks to declining corporate-tax rates,
new tax breaks, and gaping loopholes. In 1989, the latest

year for which statistics are available, 118,000 profitable companies paid no tax on profits of $25 billion.

Under the Tories the share of federal revenue from corporate taxes was halved, from 17 to less than 9 percent. If corporate taxes had grown at the same rate as sales and personal taxes, they would have brought in an extra $9 billion in 1990.

The most recent available data (either 1988 or 1989) show that, for example:

- 15 Bronfman-owned companies paid tax of less than 0.5 percent on a collective profit of $1.598 billion;
- Paul Desmarais's Power Corp. paid no taxes on profits of $215 million;
- Xerox Canada paid no taxes on profits of $106.3 million;
- Fletcher Challenge paid no taxes on profits of $119 million;
- Montreal Trust paid 1.7 percent tax on profits of $80.5 million;
- Repap Enterprises paid no taxes on profits of $176 million;
- C.P. Hotels paid no taxes on profits of $47 million;
- SNC Group paid no taxes on profits of $21 million;
- Dominion Textile paid no taxes on profits of $7 million.

All are members of the BCNI and big contributors to the Conservative party.

Shortly after the corporations secured the free-trade deal, they began a campaign to reduce the deficit and curtail social programs. This campaign, now at a fever pitch, has been successful thanks to their influence over the media. Never mentioned, however, is the role that lavish tax subsidies for corporations and the wealthy have played in the current fiscal crisis.

Here are a few:

1. The Tories brought in a $500,000 lifetime capital-gains exemption in their 1985 budget (later lowered to $100,000). This tax subsidy benefits taxpayers who realize gains on their investments. This tax is costing the Treasury $1.7 billion per year. One-half of this windfall goes to the richest 1 percent of Canadians. One-half of capital gains registered in 1990 came from real-estate speculation.

This same Conservative government slapped a ceiling on social-assistance transfer payments — money for welfare payments to Ontario, British Columbia, and Alberta — and has extended this freeze to 1995. Half of Canada's poor live in these provinces, and welfare rolls are burgeoning because of Tory policies. Such rampant greed by the government is destroying what is decent in this country. It is saving the Treasury $340 million this year.

2. In 1987, the government lowered the highest federal income-tax rate from 34 to 29 percent to harmonize with the U.S. tax system, in preparation for free trade. This is costing the Treasury $1.8 billion a year.

3. The government has maintained the entertainment-tax deduction, which allows business to deduct lunches, parties, and box seats at SkyDome. The United States has a similar loophole. This is costing

the Treasury $1 billion per year ($1.1 billion was cut from health care in 1990).

4. The 1990 budget raised the tax-deductible limits for Retirement Savings Plan contributions for high-income earners from $7,500 to $15,500. Only those earning $40,000 or more benefit from the higher limits. Only those earning $86,000 per year and over qualify for the maximum deduction. For those earning less than $40,000, the tax-deductible contribution was reduced. This retirement subsidy to the rich is costing the Treasury $350 million a year. The government's old-age security and family-allowance clawbacks are bringing in $500 million a year.

Clearly a major portion of the shortfall in government revenue is because of these tax reductions to big business and the wealthy. The government's free-trade–driven high-interest policy, which increased interest payments on the debt and increased the deficit, has masked an assault on federal spending. When the Tories came to power, federal spending was 19 percent of total spending in the economy. It is now down to 16 percent. The Tories' goal is to get it down to 14 percent in the next three years. If spending had remained at 19 percent, there would have been $20 billion more a year available for these programs. According to Arthur Kroeger, one of Ottawa's most senior bureaucrats, the government plan is that "the federal public service would be reduced to approximately one-half its present size . . . by the early part of the next century."

A Statistics Canada study released in June 1991 proves that the Conservative/corporate claim that "rampant social program spending" is responsible for the government's current financial mess is unfounded. An unpublished version of this study assigns specific blame for Canada's $400 billion debt: 44 percent is the result of the cumulative effect of tax breaks granted by Liberal and Tory governments since 1975 to corporations and the rich; 50 percent is the result of interest payments incurred by borrowing to finance deficits; and a mere 6 percent of the debt is the result of social spending. A more diplomatic version of the study, the one that was published, draws the same conclusion but in a kinder, gentler fashion: revenue shortfalls caused by tax subsidies for the rich and the corporations and charges on the resulting debt are responsible. Social spending is not the culprit. Yet, when Wilson moved to correct the revenue shortfall in 1987 he did so by increasing taxes on the middle class, not by taxing the culprits.

The StatsCan study removes the illusion of the emperor's clothes. The Conservatives and the corporate sector are guilty of trying to con Canadians into believing that they can no longer afford their social programs; in fact, it is government policy that is to blame for our financial woes.

The Goods and Services Tax was brought in as part of the free-trade agenda. It would, the Tories said, make Canadian exports more competitive. The GST, unlike the tax it was replacing, wouldn't apply to exports, but it would make up for tariff revenue lost under free trade. Why gouge average Canadians? Because, the government said, free trade made it difficult to increase income taxes above U.S. levels; therefore it had few options for increasing revenues.

They said the GST would bring in $18 billion, the same amount as the tax it replaced; the latest government estimates are that it will bring in $24 billion in its first year.

They said it would ultimately bring down inflation and that there would be a one-time increase of 1.25 percent. In fact, when the GST was implemented in January 1991, inflation increased by 2.6 percent. The annual rate was pushed up to 6.8 percent, the highest since 1983. Its spinoff effects will probably last a couple of years.

They said the poor would be protected by the GST tax credit, should they apply (one million have not). Like earlier Tory tax tricks, these are false promises. The Canadian Consumers' Association released a study in May 1991 that found that the price of thirty-six of fifty-two items surveyed "either went up more or down less than the government had estimated." Could it be that the corporations are not passing on the savings they received from the removal of the old manufacturers' sales tax?

The GST is merely the most visibly offensive manifestation of the Conservative corporate drive to refashion a meaner, crueller Canada in the new continental order.

4.

THE ATTACK ON CULTURE

*"The prospect of pain must be inserted into the
equation, else the solution will never be suitable."*
— Jack Valenti,
of the American Motion Picture Export Association

CANADIAN CULTURE IS A POLITICAL LIA-
bility in the new world order. Every country has a culture
or cultures as expressed by its writers, poets, dancers,
musicians, painters, and filmmakers; and many, especially
smaller countries, actively support cultural industries in
order to foster a vibrant national environment for the arts.
In young and sparsely populated Canada, it has been essential that the government support the creation of a Canadian culture, to express values and history that reflect our
country and to retain a sense of separateness crucial to our
survival as a nation. Without public support, Canadian
culture could not survive.

Yet, at the very time an independent cultural industry is
more important than ever, given declining Canadian economic sovereignty, the Mulroney government is starving
or shutting down whole sectors of our cultural life. This is
a government with no national vision of the country other

than the bottom line; therefore it perceives no identity for which to fight.

Quite simply, Canada cannot have an independent, publicly funded voice in a monolithic corporate-driven North American trade and military zone. And it cannot afford Canadian culture when it is trying to replace it with a new "win or die" national identity.

Canadian culture is threatened in three ways: American and international challenges to Canada's right to foster an independent cultural industry as a complement to culture from other countries; decentralization of federal powers to the provinces; and deep cutbacks to funding by a government determined to bring a market mentality to the arts.

Free-Trade Threat

The American government and entertainment industries are on record that they are determined to remove all cultural protection in Canadian law. The status quo in the cultural industries, including broadcasting, was generally exempt from the provisions of the Canada-U.S. Free Trade Agreement; however, the "standstill" clause prohibits the Canadian government from acting to diminish the current high levels of foreign ownership and control of our cultural creativity. Nor can Canada regulate new developments in cultural technology.

The deal gives the United States important new powers over Canadian culture. It established, for the first time in Canada, a commercial definition of culture, which is foreign to Canada's history (and used nowhere else in the world except the United States). This new definition is fundamental to the internal pressures being felt by the arts community in Canada today as it struggles to survive under a new, Americanized system of values. Any change to this definition is subject to negotiations with the United States.

In addition, the United States has the right to retaliate against any negative economic impact on U.S. communications or entertainment industries caused by Canadian regulatory, tax, or fiscal policies in the cultural sector by taking measures "of equivalent commercial effect" in other sectors of the economy. In other words, our vulnerable textile, lumber, or steel industries could be pitted for survival against our writers and film producers.

Weak as Canada's deal is in its ability to serve Canadian interests, it is working against the U.S. agenda; for the Canada-U.S. Free Trade Agreement is the prototype for future U.S. deals, and its terms are closely scrutinized by other countries. At the GATT talks, culture and the burgeoning information industry are shaping up as major economic and trade issues. The United States is seeking international corporate free trade in these sectors and is being met with stiff opposition from many GATT countries. They argue that Canada's culture exemption is a precedent and are demanding similar protection. The United States is determined to solve the dispute by removing the Canadian "irritants."

The exemption of culture from the free-trade agreement was a very contentious and very public issue; immediately after the signing of the free-trade deal, the United States made it clear that culture was going to be a key concern to be discussed in future talks. The president of the United States issued a two-year study of the impact of the free-trade agreement, made public in early 1991. He clearly signalled further negotiations on this subject: "Canadian actions to enforce the investment restrictions in the cultural sectors create irritants in bilateral relations."

U.S. trade representative Carla Hills has launched several strong attacks on Canadian culture, including the Canadian legislation that disallows tax deductions for advertising in U.S. magazines sold in Canada. She is further "irritated" by Canadian-content rules for TV, simultaneous substitution of Canadian commercials on U.S. programs, public subsidies to the CBC and Telefilm Canada, and policies that support Canadian ownership of book and newspaper publishing.

She appears to have been heard in Ottawa on this last concern. In 1990, finance minister Michael Wilson wrote a letter to culture minister Marcel Masse in which he made plain his dislike for the "Baie Comeau Policy." Under this policy, Investment Canada is supposed to ensure that, when a book-publishing company changes hands, Canadians must retain 51 percent control. Said Wilson, "This requirement runs counter to the government's open-for-business philosophy, has the potential to be very costly in the future, and could pose a continuing irritant to our relations with the United States."

The U.S. television and film industry is lobbying heavily to kill the Canadian cultural trade exemption in the upcoming trilateral negotiations. Canada's remaining protections represent a precedent detrimental to the American Motion Picture Export Association's attempts to institute world-wide free trade for Hollywood movies. It has already won a partial victory: Canada backed down over long-promised legislation to increase Canadian control in film distribution.

Now the U.S. government has assured the American motion picture industry that the Canada-U.S. deal will be subsumed to the new three-way agreement. Julius Katz, Carla Hills's deputy, says that the new negotiations will "broaden and liberalize . . . go beyond wherever we can."

He has specifically said that the exemption for Canada's cultural industries in the Canada-U.S. deal won't be granted in the trilateral deal with Mexico. Says Hills, "We strongly believe that cultural exemptions are restrictive and protectionist." Canada's insistence on keeping cultural protections would be "a very big mistake."

A close reading of Hills's words explains the American view of culture as entertainment. In the United States, cultural activity conforms to the spirit of entrepreneurship so embedded in American society and is expected to be competitive in and of itself. The commercialization of Canadian culture is a direct U.S. goal in trade negotiations. Says Hills, "I think Canada can protect its culture in all sorts of ways. It can have cultural support fairs and communications and that sort of thing."

The day that the U.S. Senate Finance Committee gave its approval of trilateral free-trade talks, film-industry lobby chief Jack Valenti rejoiced, but warned that if Canada insists on keeping its cultural protections, he will lobby to have Canada thrown out of the talks. The United States is now proposing revisions to visa regulations governing visits of foreign artists.

Robert Everett-Green of *The Globe and Mail* points out that the U.S. Immigration and Naturalization Service plans to set a quota on the number and length of visas granted, and to refuse entry to members of ensembles who have been affiliated with their group for less than a year. The effects of these measures could be very serious for Canadian artists. The time limit of ninety days will unnerve some managers of large organizations, who will not want to see a tour three years in the planning fall apart. The requirement of a year's membership in a performing ensemble could severely restrict the ability of major Canadian artistic organizations to visit the United States, as

personnel are continually changing in symphony orchestras and ballet companies. These revisions are likely to
be used as a bargaining tool to force Canada to comply
with the U.S. desire to drop the cultural exemption. Moreover, the U.S. visa proposals are unmatched on the Canadian side and, given our government's weak bargaining
history, are likely to remain so.

Says Everett-Green:

> The U.S. action is unvarnished protectionism in the
> cultural sector, the very thing the Americans claim to be
> irritated about. That, of course, is why they're doing it.
> When trade bargaining fails to satisfy, tit for tat is the
> rule, and the United States knows we are vulnerable.
> When the ramifications of the new visa regulations sink
> in, Canadian performers are going to start complaining
> to the federal government to win relief. It doesn't take
> any great political smarts to see that, in Washington,
> any such relief is likely to be tied to dilution of Canadian
> protectionist measures.

The politics of fear that drove the first talks will be even
greater this time, and Canada's ability or even desire to
protect culture at the trilateral negotiations is doubtful.

The Federal Government Bows Out
The Canadian government has informed the arts community that it is withdrawing federal support. The 1991
budget announced a cut of 40 percent, i.e., more than $1
billion, from the $2.5 billion currently spent on grants and
contributions that fund this community, among others.
Hard hit will be many of Canada's premier theatre and
dance companies, art galleries, and museums. All over
Canada, museums and galleries have been forced to cut

back on staff, programs, and hours of operation. Some, such as the Emily Carr Gallery in Victoria, may have to close permanently. Others, such as the Art Gallery of Hamilton and the London Regional Art Gallery, are in deep financial trouble. Alberta's Glenbow Museum, for example, has cut back visiting hours and access to its archives in order to pay for its security service.

Funding agencies such as the Canada Council are likely to be hardest hit and will, in turn, affect the artists and writers of our country. The Canada Council was a major player in the creation of a strong and vibrant Canadian arts community. Since its formation in 1957, it has nurtured hundreds of young companies. It now helps 197 theatres, 31 orchestras, 164 publishers, 35 dance companies, 65 film and video organizations, 50 artists' centres, 80 public galleries, and 100 cultural periodicals. Most of these did not exist when the council was formed.

Yet, not only are the council's clients being hit by these budget cuts, the council itself has had its grants capped for four years in a row. In real dollars, the operating grants of the council have shrunk by 20 percent. The Canadian Conference of the Arts, a strong supporter of the council, is not convinced the organization will be able to survive in the long term.

More insidious, however, is the federal government committee of deputies that has been instructed to determine which sectors and institutions now under federal jurisdiction can be shifted to the provinces. (As we will see in chapter 5, the new political structure of the cabinet defines all government departments, agencies, and programs to their value in terms of competition and decentralization. Any sector not considered profitable or potentially profitable will be starved, passed to a lower jurisdiction, or destroyed.)

This committee of deputies is seriously considering de-centralizing large sectors of culture; the Canada Council, as the primary funding body, is at the top of their list. Without a national guiding funding body for the arts, Canada's cultural life could return to the pre-council days, and few writers, filmmakers, and artists would be able to survive in the small Canadian market. Canadians will have little alternative but to turn increasingly to U.S. films, books, and television for their world-view.

The CBC Targeted

It is against this political backdrop that we must examine the Mulroney government's war on our cultural institutions, best exemplified by its treatment of the Canadian Broadcasting Corporation. Recent cuts to the regional programming of the CBC have left eleven production centres closed or drastically reduced and 1,100 employees without jobs. These cuts are hitting some communities very hard. The Toronto French-language TV station, which had served the majority of Ontario's 500,000 francophones, is gone. Goose Bay, Labrador, is losing all local programming; it now has no local TV source, no regional newspaper, and no ready access to other Canadian news sources. Goose Bay has been hit as well by government cutbacks to rail, air, and postal services. As a long-time resident points out, nowhere in Labrador can one see the Canadian flag flying over a Canadian institution. The CBC TV station in Windsor, Ontario, was the only Canadian television station in the area to provide local daily news coverage. All "local" programming now comes from Detroit.

Radio-Canada International has had its budget almost halved, necessitating layoffs of half the staff and a greatly reduced service. Of the fourteen languages in which the service was broadcast, only five will continue. Germany and Japan, our biggest trading partners after the United States, will no longer receive Canada's voice.

These cuts came after years of budget freezes; and another massive cut is expected. CBC employees believe that the heart will finally be cut out of the corporation. It is blatant hypocrisy for the government to enact in the recently passed Broadcast Act a mandate for the CBC to provide "a public service essential to the maintenance and enhancement of national identity and cultural sovereignty" and then deliberately to prevent the organization from fulfilling it. Given the current national and international challenges facing Canada, the removal of local and regional production and news services at the CBC amounts to unilateral cultural disarmament at the very time when Canada requires renewed commitment to cultural protection and development.

The government says that the CBC is just taking its share of deficit reduction. This is simply not so. The CBC is being deliberately targeted. If the federal expenditure budget had received cuts proportional to the last round of CBC cuts, it would have lost $10 billion dollars, and 35,000 public servants would have lost their jobs. The CBC is being targeted because it stands as the most significant symbol of an independent Canadian voice on the North American continent and is, therefore, an anachronism or worse in the world-view of this government. Even Margaret Thatcher, in her unprecedented drive to privatize all aspects of the British economy, social programs, and culture, understood that the BBC was crucial to British culture and not only protected it, but indexed it to full inflation and cost of living.

In a futile attempt to ward off cuts, senior CBC management went out of its way to pander to the government. The basic policy manual of the corporation, the *Journalistic Policy Handbook*, was revised to guarantee "balance" in all CBC programming. This has been interpreted by many journalists and interviewers at the CBC as a restriction on their ability to criticize government policy — which any good journalists consider fundamental to their jobs, no matter who is in power — and a warning not to air too many views contrary to the government "line."

Corporation employees are now expected to give equal time to both sides of an argument even when they believe that justified criticism of the government is in order. Many quietly talk of subtle censorship that influences not only their choice of guests and experts but their ability to speak on issues of the day. Elly Alboim, the senior CBC TV news producer in Ottawa, aired his concerns about the government's political motives underlying the Meech Lake Accord at an academic conference, to which he was an invited speaker. His speech was discussed at a CBC Board of Directors' meeting and he was publicly reprimanded. It has now been made clear that CBC employees are not to air personal political views at public events.

CBC staff see the reprimand as a lesson to them all: if the CBC brass can publicly circumscribe someone as senior as Alboim, they can do it to anyone. Many feel that the policy manual violates the Charter of Rights and Freedoms; but the pressure to conform to the new rules are pervasive.

However, such self-censorship by CBC management will not stop the government attack on the corporation. In fact, it will make it more vulnerable. The less relevant the corporation becomes to the real needs of Canadians, the less likely they are to fight for its survival. The CBC has been the crucial element in the development of a separate Canadian voice and must continue to serve the interests of all Canadians. To do less is to put its very existence in question.

Film Industry in Crisis

Canada's independent film industry is doomed if this government's policies continue. ACTRA has released a report that predicts a bleak future for the film and television production industry under free trade. Author Paul Audley says the industry had been experiencing tremendous growth throughout the 1980s. It came to an abrupt halt after the free-trade deal was signed in 1989, when the federal government cut the Capital Cost Allowance, a key program that promoted private investment in Canadian productions through tax breaks for investors. Many are convinced this tax incentive was bargained away in the free-trade deal.

As part of the free-trade agreement, Canada's cable-television companies have been ordered to pay $50 million a year in royalties to program producers; only 15 percent will go to Canadian producers. The industry is fighting back claiming that the amount ordered is arbitrary and serves only U.S. interests. The cabinet, which could intervene, refuses to do so. It could alter the distribution formula, enabling more royalties to go to Canadian producers, and still be fair to American companies who have royalty rights. Instead, it is allowing the free-trade deal to entrench an unbalanced system.

The government has also retreated from long-promised legislation to challenge the domination of our film-distribution industry by American companies. ACTRA's study describes this cowardice as "an unofficial ceiling on public support for Canadian production [which] was the price of the free trade agreement."

The study predicts as much as a 25 percent decline in
Canadian independent production in the early 1990s. The
budget for Telefilm Canada has been capped until at least
1995–96; this will diminish the important role of this
agency in the production and distribution of Canadian
films and television programs and further weaken the
already sagging production industry.

Cutbacks to the CBC will force Canadian TV producers
to seek more American co-producers. Such programs will
meet CBC Canadian-content guidelines but will be produced for the American market: productions will have to
be not identifiably Canadian, so they will sell in the
United States. In exchange, Canadian taxpayers will be
entitled to pay for the privilege of subsidizing American
productions through the CBC and Telefilm, and to be
served an increasingly Americanized TV diet.

The home-video market, like film distribution, is heavily dominated by U.S. corporate interests. Canadian films
have difficulty finding space on video-outlet shelves: they
are often placed in the foreign-film section. The Canadian
Film and Television Production Association warns that
this wholesale domination of our culture must end or the
country will not survive, culturally or politically. If we fail
to act soon, "foreign commercial interests will surely see
that our broadcasting system becomes integrated into a
continental system within 20 years."

Ad Industry Moves South
The cultural exemption in the free-trade agreement does
not extend to commercials; all duty from commercials
filmed by U.S. companies will be phased out by 1993.
Multinational ad agencies are consolidating commercial
production in the United States, even for ads designed
solely for the Canadian market. Canadian companies, try-

ing to compete in style and content, are hiring American actors and directors, or even subcontracting entire projects to American companies. Commercial production in Canada dropped 30 percent in 1990, and free trade has accelerated the multinational takeover of Canadian ad agencies.

The Toronto Star has documented several instances of this loss. Molson Canadian drinkers on TV are really Americans, drinking beer in the United States. Vicks Formula 44 hires an American actor for its latest ad. Canadian Goodyear's campaign uses American comedian Thom Sharpe. Ronalds-Reynolds ad agency uses American children for a Kleenex ad that runs only in Ontario. Canadian Airlines uses American actors for not only key roles, but some of the weary air travellers waiting for the Dawn of Civilization. No Canadian production house was asked to bid on the contract, and the voiceover is done by San Francisco-based Hal Riney, who is also the voice for Gallo wine. Half the production work was done in the United States, and the editor of the entire campaign is an American.

Labatt's new non-sexist Blue commercials were directed by an American on the U.S. west coast. McDonald's ads for the Canadian market host Americans playing Mr. Fish and Mr. Chicken. Canadian Tire shoots its ads in the United States, with an American director. The Toronto Transit Commission uses American director Greg Gould for its latest ads. Even the GST ads produced by the Canadian government used a GST-exempt American voiceover!

This last example is particularly galling when we assess the damage done to the industry by the GST. It may well be the final blow to the industry. Americans working in Canada on U.S. or Canadian productions do not have to charge the producer GST on their fees. Canadians working on any production made in Canada must charge GST to the producer and, under certain circumstances, must charge it on scripts submitted to the United States.

Similarly, broadcasters must charge advertisers GST on top of their fees only if the commercial is produced in Canada. If the commercial is produced in the United States and brought into Canada for broadcast under the free-trade agreement, no GST is required. The 7 percent advantage to producing in the United States is clear.

The Canadian industry is rapidly disappearing; without direct action by the government, industry officials, and the CRTC — which places no Canadian-content rules on television commercials — it will die. If our own products are being sold to us by an ad agency that sees no fundamental difference between a consumer in Newfoundland and one in Manhattan, one more source of Canadian identity will disappear. Says Martin Doyle, an ACTRA spokesperson, "If they want Canada to be the 51st state, get on with it; but this painful sort of erosion is just that. We're going to wake up one day and all our images are going to be American."

Canadian Publishers Fight for Life
Canadian-owned book publishers are in a fight for life. Several influential companies have gone under and several more are near bankruptcy. Publishers' sales dropped 30 percent in 1990, and the first half of 1991 was disastrous for the industry. Says the executive-director of the Canadian Book Publishers' Council, Jacqueline Hushion, "I have never seen it like this," noting that the 1982 recession didn't have near the impact of this recession. Industry leaders are unanimous in their dire warnings of the serious nature of this situation. A Price-Waterhouse study found that six of Canada's foremost companies are carrying

heavy deficits. Most are cutting the number of Canadian books they publish and printing fewer copies of those they choose to publish.

Without major government intervention, which is most unlikely given the trilateral trade talks and the U.S. political anger any intervention would attract, many publishing houses are going to go under, and with them the opportunities for Canadian writers, novelists, and poets to be published. Although Canadian-owned companies account for only about 20 percent of the English-language books sold in Canada, they publish over 80 percent of Canadian authors. Their crisis is more than just the individual tragedies of the companies that are going under and the people who work for them. Canada may be left without a publishing infrastructure interested in publishing the thoughts, views, and analyses of Canadians.

Only foreign-owned publishers are not in crisis currently, and these competitors have the advantage of being able to cut back on their Canadian publishing programs in tough times and rely on lower-cost books imported from their corporate parents abroad. Doubleday Canada has laid off forty-eight employees of their book-club division — a 40 percent staff reduction — and shifted responsibility for the selection of Canadian titles to a book-club editor in New York. Grolier Inc., a Connecticut-based children's and educational book publisher, has closed its Canadian direct-marketing operations and is reducing the staff of its Canadian subsidiary by one-third, a loss of ninety jobs. And Random House will be distributing all of its products, except for a few Canadian titles, from its U.S. warehouse.

This crisis is not confined to book publishers. Magazines in Canada, 300 in all, are an endangered species. More than half are just breaking even or losing money. A recent study of Canadian magazines found that they had suffered a sharp drop in advertising revenue in 1990. In the first four months of 1991 alone, ad revenues had dropped 22 percent from their already low 1990 levels.

As it is, nine out of ten magazines sold in Canada are foreign-owned; most are American. But the Canadian government is doing little to support the industry. The GST and the end to postal subsidies are crucial losses for magazines. Bill C-58, which grants tax breaks to Canadian businesses that advertise in Canadian magazines, is under attack from the United States. Moreover, the Mulroney government is not monitoring or enforcing the existing legislation. According to Doris Anderson, former editor of *Chatelaine*, U.S. magazines get around the legislation by having international and U.S. advertisers with Canadian branch plants pay for ads through their U.S. firms. About $8 million a year is lost by the Canadian industry through this loophole.

The Future of Culture
Culture is vital to defining Canadian values and distinct characteristics. Film and television have emerged as the world's most pervasive influences on the attitudes and values in most nations. We control so little that flows through our airwaves: 97 percent of screen time shows imported films; 89 percent of earnings in the sound-recording industry accrues to twelve foreign-controlled firms; 90 percent of television drama presentations are non-Canadian in origin. We also lack control over distribution, with the result that even when Canadians produce quality materials — and they do — these products do not find their way into the homes and hearts of the population.

The government obviously has no fundamental problem with this state of affairs and is now intent on destroying the few remaining ties between it and Canada's artists.

This is folly. The withdrawal of government from culture makes inevitable the eventual loss of a national cultural identity and the reduction of Canada to a mere economic arrangement. We will have no underlying sense of identity or values.

Says Keith Kelly of the Canadian Conference of the Arts, without government support for the arts, "Canada would cease to be a nation and would become a corporation." The cultural vacuum will prove a sympathetic environment for the credo for the twenty-first century, "Win or die."

There is another crucial economic dimension to this issue. Canada's economy is shifting away from manufacturing. If we do not develop a high-technology, information-based economy, we will lose the most promising economic option open to us. Information industries include books, magazines, films, records, tapes, compact discs, communication technologies, hardware and software, and other forms of cultural materials. Says the Canadian Conference of the Arts, the real emphasis will be on software, the very stuff of the cultural sector. "Carriers need content — content is the cultural sector."

The information age rewards creativity and innovation, hallmarks of the cultural sector. The cultural labour force in Canada, the fastest-growing sector of the economy, is 400,000 strong and of strategic importance to our economic future. It cannot be left to chance or, worse, cut off from national purpose and nation-building.

Technological changes are sweeping through broadcasting and media around the world. Satellites are scheduled for launch over the next few years that will girdle the earth with signals powerful enough to provide fully interactive, direct-to-home services, in addition to direct broadcasts.

According to the Canadian Film and Television Production Association, Canada will be one of the first countries to be exposed to this damage, as U.S. satellites come
on stream in 1992 with direct-to-home services. Enormous satellites dishes will soon be a thing of the past. Small
receivers, the size of a page, will permit Canadians to tap
into this new, unlimited broadcast feast.

A service called SkyPix will be launched from the
United States this year, with eighty channels, including up
to fifty pay-per-view channels with movies starting every
fifteen minutes. SkyCable, with more than a hundred
channels, will be operational by 1993. The vast majority of
our population will be able to receive them. Canadians
will soon gain access to hundreds of channels featuring
non-Canadian services by purchasing an inexpensive piece
of receiving equipment.

Fears for the survival of a Canadian industry in the face
of this onslaught are very real. Under the free-trade agreement, Canada can take no new action to protect Canadian
culture from this inundation, nor can the government
guarantee to provide more Canadian cultural products to
enable the industry to compete. In fact, the government
has actively decided to "co-operate" in the U.S. information revolution by tearing down Canadian barriers to its
success.

Perhaps the most sinister aspect of this capitulation is
that when our cultural voice goes, our independent, critical, political voice is silenced as well. The Mulroney government has given away our economic sovereignty; it has
abandoned our commitment to a social safety network; it
has created a continental energy pool in which the United
States has as much claim to our resources as does Canada.
Now, it is cutting the vocal chords of dissent.

Economic acquiescence is only half the story in the creation of this continent-wide trade and military block. Political acquiescence is equally crucial. Says documentary-film researcher Colleen Fuller, "Americans have long understood that U.S. penetration of the international cultural sphere would enable them to better control and influence the political discourse in other countries." The result, for Canada, is a country reshaped to fit George Bush's new world order.

To Save an Industry
An industrial strategy for our cultural and high-technology sector must be an economic and cultural priority. We must actively promote Canadian-originated services in Canada, assert our clear intention to remain a sovereign and separate nation through our communications strategy, create new methods and forms of program production, and take control of the sources of distribution of cultural products in Canada. None of this can be done under the existing free-trade arrangement. Nor can we create a national cultural vision, which is so badly needed in our divided nation.

We need to build relationships with countries outside North America, and to market our products there. We need a national policy and strategy for the creation, production, and distribution of cultural materials and services. We have a strong and vibrant cultural sector ready to advise government on the specifics of this policy, and it must be consulted widely. A fragmented system of cultural promotion will fail.

What could Canada promote? Like all nations, Canada can best promote what we Canadians have lived: an aboriginal population with a rich and varied history; two founding nations, struggling to survive side by side; and a truly multiracial population striving to discover the true meaning of tolerance in an increasingly intolerant world. D. Paul Schafer, director of the Canadian arm of the UNESCO-sponsored World Culture Project, poses this question: if Canada has evolved a culture over the centuries that is ordered differently than the cultures of other countries and, by virtue of this evolution, radiates a distinctive set of characteristics, what contributions can this culture make to national development?

He answers that Canadian culture must be indigenous, that is it should grow organically out of the roots, soil, and traditions of the country's own cultural experiences rather than through imitation of the cultural experiences of other countries. Practically, this means accepting the fact that the origins and roots of Canadian cultures are first aboriginal, then European. "Not only does this mean recognizing the Indians and Inuit as the founding peoples of Canadian culture and rewriting our history books accordingly, but also it means empowering the native people to take control of their own cultural development and destiny."

Culture must be egalitarian, not restricted to Canadians of a certain social status or educational background. Rather, Canadian culture is every Canadian's birthright; participating in our cultural expression every Canadian's reality. This is very different from the passive role of most "viewers" of current North American entertainment.

Moreover, Schafer states, it is through reuniting Canadians with their natural environment that our culture should be nurtured. We have grown away from the earth, and in so doing, have become the most wasteful people in the world. We must become finely attuned to the realities of nature, instead of building policies and practices based on separation from nature. Similarly, we must rediscover unity through equality and diversity. Our search for answers to these most difficult questions may be our best export.

He asks, "Wouldn't we be better off to persevere with the creation of a society based on tolerance, pluralism, and respect for the rights of others — even if this means more social, ethnic, and linguistic tensions and demands for sovereignty association — than to settle for a society based on intolerance, assimilation, totalitarianism, and suppression of the rights of others?" Through such a definition of culture might come the answers to our constitutional crisis.

The need for a national cultural policy with a strong commitment to the growth of an information industry in Canada is urgent. Says the Canadian Film and Television Production Association, "We look to the federal government for strong, intelligent, nationalistic leadership. If it is not forthcoming, our industry will work to develop its own strategy for survival, which will rely substantially on the survival of Canada."

This government must understand how serious Canadians are about protecting their heritage. If the federal government will not act, the people of Canada must. We first need to claim responsibility for our cultural lives and place these issues high on our policy agenda. This government must be held accountable to the Canadian people for any destruction of our heritage.

5.

THE PERVERSION OF THE POLITICAL PROCESS

"We have every intention of restructuring Canada."

— Brian Mulroney

THE SYSTEMATIC DESTRUCTION OF A nation is no easy feat. Contriving its economic dependence on a foreign power is an important first step, but it must be accompanied by strong internal changes to destabilize and reduce federal structures and powers.

Canada is facing one of its most important constitutional tests of nationhood. Tragically for Canada, negotiating on the federal side is a government clearly prepared to sell the country's heritage for the power and favour of its big-business friends. A close examination of the constitutional deal-making so far reveals that the Mulroney government is using the crisis with Quebec to further its own economic ends: our constitutional problems have become a wonderful opportunity to dose all of Canada with Tory medicine.

Business Takes Charge

The business and political elite that privately fashioned a free-trade deal with the United States — the alliance that is selling off Canada's heritage, privatizing its essential services, and destroying universality — has a new cause. They tell us Canada cannot compete internationally, not because of bungling Tory policies but because we are burdened with too much government — too many overlapping levels and jurisdictions and too many federal responsibilities to the provinces. The solution? Dump powers now vested at the federal level on other levels of government. The code words of the campaign are "competitiveness" and "decentralization"; and the government is responding by linking the two in a way reminiscent of its response to early corporate demands for free trade.

Says Du Pont Canada chairman J.E. Newall, a strong free-trade supporter, "As a nation, we are overgoverned." While maintaining that the federal government should be made stronger in ways that will increase Canadian competitiveness, Newall calls for the elimination of most other federal involvement. "The primary determinant for change must be to improve our economic performance . . . with a strong bias to decentralization wherever possible."

The Business Council on National Issues is once again chief promoter of the cause. It hosted a symposium on the Constitution in early 1991 and produced a volume of research strongly backing a massive redistribution of federal powers. Based on the groundless premise that economic interests are "the only ties that still bind Canadians," the BCNI concludes that the large corporations will "play a decisive role" in resolving the constitutional impasse and that it is the force that should reply to Quebec on behalf of Canada.

The Canadian Chamber of Commerce's Tim Reid

agrees: "You've got to design a Constitution that makes sense in terms of the rough and tough international competitive environment we are moving into."

Jack Masterman, chairman of The Mutual Group, says, "A revitalized Canada requires . . . a more decentralized federation." Bank of Nova Scotia chairman Cedric Ritchie is even more outspoken. "We need nothing less than a complete rethink of the mission statement of the public sector. Canadians can no longer afford . . . habitual reliance on government."

Think tanks that the Mulroney government holds in high esteem — the Institute for Research on Public Policy, the C.D. Howe Institute, the Economic Council of Canada, and the Fraser Institute — have been influenced by the new "competitiveness" gurus Joseph D'Cruz and Alan Rugman of the University of Toronto, and Harvard professor Michael Porter. D'Cruz and Rugman argue that the costs of government services in Canada must be benchmarked by those in the United States: with free trade, it is the only way we can compete.

The Fraser Institute advocates the transfer of public funds for education and health from the provinces to individuals. This would give public services competition from the private sector. It would allow the government to decide, probably by means testing, who has a right to these services — they would no longer be universal. It would also open the doors to private-enterprise education and health care in Canada. This would be good, proponents argue, because, through the natural laws of the marketplace, the public service would be reduced or made redundant.

Michael Walker, the Fraser Institute head, applauds the government's intention to legislate a ceiling on all government spending, as was done recently in the United States:

"Legislated restraint on the size of government is a tremendous idea." He denounces the "coercive" nature of national social programs and says that, without national "dictates," the provinces could deliver these programs more effectively, i.e., privately.

Says Harvey Enchin of *The Globe and Mail*:

Canada's captains of competitiveness are advocating changes that would transform the country as dramatically as anything envisaged by Quebec's separatist zealots.

Continental north-south trade flows would supersede cross-Canada trade, despite the removal of interprovincial barriers. Canada's costly, cumbersome three-tier government would be rationalized — perhaps replaced — by a streamlined system delivering whatever public services would remain through the regional level, close to consumers. Federal transfer payments would be curtailed, as income redistribution would no longer be appropriate government policy. Official bilingualism, marketing boards and regulatory agencies — all hindrances to competitiveness — would be phased out.

Toronto venture capitalist Gordon Sharwood says it most honestly: "The only cloud in this [competitiveness] ointment is that the electorate . . . are strongly resistant to competitive pressures and are much more interested in a caring society."

Quebec's Business Elite Onside
Crucially, the corporate voices of Quebec are singing the same song. "By golly, we're overgoverned," says Jean de Grandpré, chairman emeritus of BCE. Claude Castonguay,

senator and head of the Laurentian Bank of Canada, says that a decentralized system is the best hope for keeping Canada together. He suggests that the federal government take responsibility only for economic issues relating to the country as a whole. He questions all other federal institutions, particularly that fundamental Canadian belief that services should be equal across the country. "A uniform Canada, with everybody on the same footing? I don't think it's possible."

Canadian Business magazine says that federalists are alive and well in Quebec and that they control the province's major business and financial institutions. However, it says, Quebec business leaders want radical change with massive devolution of federal powers to the regions. "Their diagnosis of Canada's constitutional malaise is no more complicated than grade-school math: the country is too integrated, the mortgage is too high, we depend on each other too much."

Quebec corporate leaders assert that leaving Canada would cost too much, make the Quebec economy very vulnerable, and create opportunities for the Quebec labour movement that would threaten the Quebec these business leaders want to build. A recent poll of the major companies in Quebec by Quebec's major corporate lobby group, Le Conseil du partronat du Québec, showed that 64 percent support federalism.

However, it is clear that the federal structure must change if federalism is to work for these leaders. Says Serge Saucier, head of Raymond Chabot, Martin Paré & Associates, the largest Quebec-based accounting firm, "We'd like business people to realize that the present formula, if unchanged, leads to no good." Like their counterparts in English-speaking Canada, these corporate leaders favour a huge reduction of the system of transfer payments to the provinces, so that provincial spending and priorities can be controlled by big-business interests.

Just as the International Monetary Fund dictates conditions of loans and debt relief to debtor countries, so the Canadian federal government, speaking for corporate concerns, will be able to call on provinces to make structural adjustments in return for more favourable terms regarding transfer payments. Head of the National Bank of Canada, André Bérard, puts it this way: "The provinces that come up short will have to make praiseworthy efforts before they can get help from the central government."

Castonguay adds, "In the future, Canadians will have to go where the jobs are. We can't go on pretending that Canadians will be able to remain in regions where job creation is difficult, and then expect to maintain a standard of living comparable to other regions."

But Quebec business cannot restructure the country alone, say influential Quebec corporate leaders. The business elite from all parts of Canada must join forces if this new vision is to succeed. "If anyone can save Canada," says Jean Paré, publisher of L'Actualité, "it's Toronto and Montreal and Canada's private sector, not Ottawa and the governments." He says that if Canadian business leaders could agree on a slate of demands, "it wouldn't take three months before it was adopted by politicians."

This theme is central to the Quebec Liberal party's constitutional document, the Allaire Report, which calls for the "radical reform of political and administrative structures of the central government." Throughout the Western world, says the document, the role of the state is being downsized. But Canada continues to hold on to national structures. "It is becoming increasingly obvious that the Canadian federal state is based on centralizing practices dictated by an inflexible will to standardize public services to the utmost and the pursuit of grand, so-called national policies."

The authors are very critical of the difficulty the federal government is encountering in passing legislation they consider crucial to the economic health of Quebec. They cite the free-trade agreement and the GST as two initiatives that are absolutely necessary to increase the country's competitiveness, and lament the way in which they were handled politically by the federal government. The problem with Canada, according to the Allaire Report, is that it is based on the concept of an interventionist, welfare state. "Market globalization requires an effective, competitive administrative machinery, while public interventionism often leads to dependence and biases the socio-economic agents."

The Allaire Report, speaking for the Quebec Liberal party, believes, like the BCNI, that only economic considerations link Canadians. It is calling for a radical change in the role of the national government. No longer will government intervene in the economy to regulate market operations in the public interest and ensure equality of services. Instead, its role will be to streamline the entire national system — economic, social, political, and cultural — to provide a welcome environment for transnational competition and investment.

"Canada must be profoundly changed," says the report. Envisaging an economic union between Quebec and Canada, and among the provinces, Allaire calls for a system in which "the citizen . . . takes his own destiny in hand. In this new context, the state becomes a facilitator."

Decentralization is the key. Individuals are on their own in a U.S.-style "facilitator" state, the business agent for those who make it to the top of the heap. Says Jean Allaire, "What is government if it is not big business?"

Danger Signals for Canada

Frances Russell of the *Winnipeg Free Press* says that the battle to save Canada isn't between Quebec and the rest of the country, between the East and the West, or between French and English. The battle to save Canada is between its elites and its citizens. As she points out, not a day goes by that we are not told that we hate government, that we think we are overgoverned, that we hate bilingualism, and that we want to see the country decentralized. Yet all the polls tell us only a minority want to see radical change to the structures that have served us for many years.

Where, then, do such false "rumours" come from? The reality is that it is the corporate elite, the forces whose policies have so devastated the country, who are revving up these engines of decentralization and competitiveness. Wherever they live, in Quebec or outside, big-business interests have more in common with one another than with ordinary people, who are being crushed by their self-serving policies.

In the name of "saving Canada," these business leaders are joining their political allies in Ottawa to diminish the federal Canadian state with a strong commitment to the welfare of all its people. Quite simply, less government is good for business. The model is American; with hemispheric free trade, gutting the federal state will create a corporate paradise.

Federal spending power has been the crucial tool with which we have built the system we have; losing it will quickly eradicate the federal government's ability to determine standards, set regulations that protect us from unscrupulous business practices, and demand practices that conserve our resources. Yet, the corporate/Tory goal is to give over jurisdiction to the provinces of all federal powers, regulatory agencies, and institutions that don't actively support competitiveness. Likely candidates for devolution are culture, bilingualism, and social programs, and the federal government is likely to offer shared jurisdiction over immigration and the environment.

The finance ministers of the four western provinces have issued a report calling for the "disentanglement" of the federal government from universal social programs. They say the provinces, governed by the principles of "affordability, efficiency, stability and simplicity," should have control of Medicare. Health minister Benoît Bouchard is very open to their views. "I'm ready to put everything on the table and readdress all the powers of the provinces and ourselves."

A group of prominent Canadians, calling themselves the "Group of 22," has floated a trial balloon for the government and its corporate agenda. The group (one of whose members, Hugh Segal, is now senior political adviser to Brian Mulroney) recommended radical restructuring of the country through massive decentralization of federal powers, including health care. They go farther than the Meech Lake Accord and the Allaire Report in providing the Mulroney government with a constitutional rationale for its competitiveness plan. Their proposal would result in weaker social programs, delivered at the provincial level; in their model, the federal government's transfer payments would be largely dictated by strategies for economic competitiveness. This would serve to further balkanize the country.

Even their basic assumption — that increasing the federal government's responsibility for economic competitiveness will result in greater prosperity — is flawed. Canada's experience with continental free trade has been just the opposite; only a very few wealthy transnationals have gained.

Competitive Poverty

Given the lack of protection for wages and social programs in the trilateral free-trade deal, it is evident that Brian Mulroney's definition of competitiveness is a third-world model. His government is slashing taxes to big — but not to small — business, pressuring working people to lower wage demands, killing social programs, cutting back on research and development, and destroying the communications and transportation infrastructures of the country by imposing on them a North-South axis.

He is hoping that such actions will attract business investment to Canada. But this model of competitiveness is the endless downward spiral of countries such as Argentina, which have a small, very wealthy business class but whose population lives in increasing impoverishment.

The balkanization of Canada is crucial to this scenario, for a weakened nation-state would leave Canada more vulnerable to increased global competition in a changing world. The decentralization of federal powers would necessitate each province developing its own social structures, its own standards, and its own regulations.

As David Crane of *The Toronto Star* points out, this could lead to provinces bidding against one another for industry, by lowering environmental or wage standards to attract investment. Nations compete this way. What would stop provinces from doing so once there is no sense of mutual responsibility and no national standards to enforce?

Ironically, a new bureaucracy would be needed to monitor the interprovincial issues that would arise from the new structure. The overseeing body would, for example, regulate cross-provincial use of social programs to prevent Canadians who live in provinces with lower standards from registering for social programs in another whose standards are superior.

This new bureaucracy would, of course, be as costly to administer as the federal structure. But those pushing for a radical shift of power do not see this irony, for all their complaints about the cost of government. For it is not government per se that corporate interests object to, but the current federal structure. Big business believes that market forces are the only forces that count, and they want to enshrine in the Constitution a radically reduced federal state, in which corporations would have much more freedom to manoeuvre. The bureaucracy to facilitate this new system is a perfectly acceptable cost, while paying for the current system is not. Similarly, the corporate backers of the GST don't seem to mind the huge and expensive bureaucracy that has been created to service the new tax. Perhaps this is because their share of the tax burden has been reduced, and they aren't paying for much of it.

A New Political Structure

To deliver this new system, two cabinet "superministries" have been established: Constitutional Affairs, under Joe Clark, and International Trade, under Michael Wilson. Clark is using his expanded federal-provincial–relations role to assure the provinces that Ottawa is preparing for substantial decentralization. Wilson and his burgeoning bureaucracy are softening up the provinces to accede to economic demands that will help the country become more "competitive."

The goals of these twin ministries of competition and decentralization take precedence over those of all other ministries. External Affairs and Finance, for instance, will be subordinated to the trade portfolio; Health and Welfare and Communications will be subordinated to the unity portfolio. From now on, all government business and all public policy will be assessed according to the blueprint of the superministries' twin goals of competition and decentralization. Any Canadian institution, practice, or law that does not promote these aims will be abolished or starved, either directly or by being passed to a lower level of government.

The Mulroney government's 1991 Throne Speech stressed the relationship between national unity and prosperity and insisted that there is more to national unity than amending the constitution. "Our unity is strengthened by a strong economy. And prosperity is enhanced by a united country. But disunity in the face of the global economic challenge invites decline." For the government, "national unity" is a commercial arrangement, not "global," but continental.

This government believes that social programs, culture, language, and environment are counterproductive, as they render Canada less competitive in the global economy. Therefore these areas will be scrutinized very carefully for components to cut and/or devolve from the federal level.

The government has already radically altered the way Canada assists developing nations. The new goal is to foster right-wing, free-market economies that will work well with international corporate free trade. A growing proportion of aid in the next decade will go to countries that, like Mexico, agree to the long-term restructuring programs demanded by the World Bank and the International Monetary Fund: privatizing state assets, lowering wages, displacing farmers from the land, devaluing the currency, slashing education and health programs, and welcoming foreign investment on any terms.

The Canadian International Development Agency proposes fundamental changes in its structure, from an emphasis on foreign-aid programs to contracting out its operations to the private sector for projects approved by the World Bank. Widespread cuts in staff are expected and a number of countries will no longer receive aid. CUSO, largely funded by CIDA, has had workers pulled from projects involving unions or groups working to improve their living conditions; and several agencies have suffered government cutbacks because, they believe, they have criticized this new policy direction. Dozens of overseas projects have been killed, and closures of whole operations in some countries are imminent. Foreign aid has fallen victim to the new theology of this government and its political masters: the world must be made safe for the transnationals.

Everywhere traditional Canadian concerns are being subordinated to the gospel of competitiveness. Canada is preparing for one of the most important international conferences ever to be held on the environment, the United Nations Conference on Environment and Development, slated to take place in Brazil in 1992. In spring 1991, the Canadian government briefed environmentalists on one aspect of the conference, the Conservation of Biological Diversity Convention. It was clear that Canada's interests are access to global genetic resources and advanced technology, and the protection and extension of plant-breeders' rights and intellectual-property safeguards. In other words, Canada will be arguing for the extension of the rights of private transnationals.

When confronted by several participants of the meeting who believe that such goals violate the meaning of the Brazil conference, Canadian officials admitted that "corporate interests are firmly entrenched in our position."

Competition Tory Style

To render Canada more competitive, the federal government will strengthen its hand in two key areas — interprovincial trade and education. No one would object to the creation of a more open trading system within Canada. In fact, for this government to have entered into a free-trade agreement with the United States before it strengthened the East-West flows within Canada was national economic suicide: American companies have national treatment rights in any province of Canada but the provinces can still discriminate against one another.

However, by opening all provincial barriers to trade, investment, and services *after* entering free trade with the United States and Mexico, the Mulroney government is consigning the less-advantaged regions and provinces to chronic poverty. North-South trade is the government's priority; it is removing interprovincial barriers in order to reduce provincial impediments to this goal. The government's policies of free trade, deregulation, and a high dollar are squeezing Canadian companies, which are forced to compete with American giants in Canada. Many Canadian companies are "rationalizing" production away from Canada; other companies will "rationalize" within Canada, shifting to large centres from "non-viable" regions such as the Atlantic provinces.

Continental free trade will be made more efficient with a single integrated Canadian market modelled on the U.S. corporate system, especially if social structures are no longer a national responsibility. Local industries that cannot compete within the new continental order will be abandoned: free trade across Canada will do to the poorer regions what free trade with the United States has done to Canada as a whole.

The Mulroney government's plan to strengthen its

powers in the area of education, a provincial jurisdiction, is more alarming. Again, national education standards are a laudable goal, if their aim is to enhance the country's integrity and standing in the world community and to improve our quality of life and productivity. But the long-term goal of the government and corporations is private-industry control of education and training.

Employment minister Bernard Valcourt was given the responsibility for the government's new national education thrust. This is significant, as the minister traditionally most closely identified with education is the secretary of state. The choice of Valcourt, linking education and employment, is a signal that the education initiative is part of the government's prosperity and competitiveness agenda. The Privy Council bureaucrat responsible for the strategy, Peter Hicks, was formerly the head of the Canadian Jobs Strategy, the Mulroney government initiative that directed job-training money from traditional educational institutions to private corporations. By considering education as training, a means of human-resource development, the government is making it clear that the purpose of education is not to educate but to serve the needs of business.

The federal government wants more control over education in order to shift the focus in Canada's schools and universities from the humanities and social sciences to the training of workers, whether tradespeople or professions, for the transnationals of tomorrow. In so doing, it is radically shifting the foundations of Canadian education and will open the doors to U.S. private institutions. Control over education spending will enable the federal government to withhold public funding from provincial policies and projects of which it disapproves and support those initiatives and programs, particularly in the private sector, that satisfy its new educational criteria of competitiveness and efficiency.

This includes the contracting out of teaching to the private sector. The federal government will delineate which areas of instruction are deemed to be provided under private employment training, and opportunities for jobs will shift from the public sector to private, largely American firms. Such jobs, quite apart from their educational aims, will not carry the security or benefits now enjoyed by Canadian educators.

In the 1991 Throne Speech, the government quadrupled funding for private training by employers while making cuts to public education. Adult-education specialist John Jackson points out that transfer-payment cuts to post-secondary education have sharply reduced Canadian universities' ability to fulfil their mandate. Having created a crisis in our universities, the government has also created an alternative, the private sector. Mainstream public education, which will remain within the provincial systems, will be starved for federal funds; business-related training will be federally controlled and well nourished with federal funds.

Private-sector educational organizations will have access to the funds provided for literacy and job training, i.e., they will become responsible for the government's new education initiative. However, says Jackson, "there is an insidious twist involved in the provision of funds under the Conservatives' 'prosperity agenda.' American universities will be able to access Canadian taxpayers' funds for business-related training — Canadian universities will not have access to the same funds. American school boards will be able to teach literacy classes to Canadian workers in Canadian factories, while Canadian school boards will not be able to spend money on such endeavours." American educational institutions will be eligible for Canadian funding because they are corporate entities, that is, private enterprises; Canadian institutions are not.

As American educational institutions expand into Canada, competition between them and Canadian institutions will increase. Canadian universities will try, probably unsuccessfully, to compete by scraping to the bone, eliminating non-practical "fringe" humanities courses, and reducing opportunities for Canadian perspectives on trade, culture, and politics.

There is already strong pressure to permit the establishment of private universities in Canada, which haven't been allowed for thirty years. Former education minister Bette Stephenson has been lobbying the Ontario government to change the law to permit private universities in the province. A well-organized and well-funded group that includes several prominent members of the former Ontario Conservative government plans to establish a private university in York Region, north of Toronto.

Most of the top schools in the United States are private, financed largely by corporations who thereby acquire huge influence on how the schools are run and what subjects and values are taught. American business schools recognize that the business community is their benefactor as well as the end consumer of their product and therefore tend not to teach their students to question the values of the corporate-driven system in which they operate.

State-supported Canadian business schools, on the other hand, do not think of students as customers or the business community as a client; but this will change. Says Roger Wolff, dean of management at the University of Toronto, "We are going to see business schools that are, if not totally privatized and almost free-standing, then very close to it." Business will call the shots, and the results for Canadian universities could be traumatic.

Once business schools are privatized, there will be enormous pressure to permit other universities and community colleges to be privatized as well. Under the spirit of free trade, private American schools will be looking to expand to Canada. The next, natural step would be for struggling or profit-minded private universities to be sold in whole or in part to corporations. As Robert Adolph, a humanities professor at York University, points out, the history of Connaught BioSciences — once part of the University of Toronto, then an independent Canadian company, ultimately sold to foreign interests — may be instructive.

"Canadian private universities, like those in the United States, would be funded by large-scale 'free enterprise.' Like most of their counterparts in the United States, their style and policies would reflect pro-business and continentalist values. This would result in increased specialization in science, business, and technology training at the expense of general, and especially humanistic, education. It could also force the establishment of an American-style two-tier system: elitist, private, prestigious universities for those who qualify academically and financially; and public universities for the less promising and the less wealthy."

The government is calling for a new "learning culture" in Canada that equates learning with competitiveness and subjects all aspects of life in Canada to this gospel: Democracy is "adjusted" to the needs of big business; individual and social rights are "adjusted" to the economic goal of becoming sufficiently lean and mean to compete with the third world.

Interestingly, the 1991 Throne Speech incursion into education was greeted amicably in Quebec. On the surface, this is surprising because education is provincial turf

and Quebec more than the other provinces guards it fero-
ciously. The Parti Québécois leader expressed anger at the
affront, saying, "It's the first time in fifty years that a
Quebec government has accepted a direct federal intrusion
in education." Several Liberal cabinet ministers objected
in politely restrained tones. But the premier, Robert
Bourassa, contends that the initiatives do not amount to an
intrusion by Ottawa into education. He understands that it
is not public education in which the federal government is
interested.

The prime minister would not have risked such a shot at
Quebec's jurisdiction without prior consent of the Quebec
business community and the premier. The business community has indicated its assent with uncharacteristic si-
lence. The prime minister purred, "I have spoken to Mr.
Bourassa, have no fear."

"There is a Canadian economic space," said Bourassa,
by way of explaining his acceptance of the initiative. "This
implies the free circulation of people, capital, goods and
services, which . . . means searching for common objectives." Bernard Valcourt added that this is not a jurisdictional issue but "about our future prosperity and our own
standard of living." Both are amazing examples of the
political art of saying nothing of substance in a clever way
about something of substance that can't be admitted.
What can't be admitted is that Bourassa's acceptance of
this incursion into Quebec's jurisdiction is an acknowledgment on his part that he has no intention of taking
Quebec out of Canada but is working with the prime
minister to take Canada into the continental market-place.
Hello, Canada Inc.

PART TWO

TAKE BACK THE NATION

6.
A Constitution for All Canadians

"Canada is the solution looking for a problem."
— Carlos Barrio Gomez,
former Mexican ambassador to Canada

THE CURRENT BATTLE BEING WAGED BY THE
political and corporate elites of Canada and Quebec on
their citizens has its roots deep in the history of our
colonial past. Canada's parliamentary system was based on
the British model, complete with a Senate that provided
special powers for an aristocratic ruling class, although
doubts were raised in the British Parliament that the notion of class could be transferred to the new colony. The
English and French carved up the country for their mutual
benefit in their early trade wars; and the aboriginal people
were used by both to fatten the coffers of the merchant
class back home.

Before Confederation, Quebec was the centre of this
struggle. The British worked with the "Canadiens"
against their major trading rivals, the Americans. Quebec,
which included the territory of present-day Ontario, was
the focus of English mercantile expansion. After Con-

federation, when Quebec and Ontario had been settled, western Canada became the new frontier. Like the French and English before them, central Canadian powers harnessed the riches of the new territory for their own benefit. Although those moving west were anglophones and non-francophone immigrants, and western expansionism aided almost exclusively the English merchant class, the expansion was launched from Montreal. This irony was not lost on Quebec.

Constitutional changes were closely aligned to the economic goals of the political and business ruling class of the expanding country. As the "two solitudes" became more deeply entrenched, the English devoted themselves to commerce; the French, ruled by the church, remained largely rural and non-entrepreneurial. The current crisis in Canada is a modern version of these power struggles, the legacy of constitutional deal-making at the expense of Quebec's legitimate rights.

The Quebec Act of 1774 was the first recognition of a distinct society in that it guaranteed French Canadians the right to their own language, civil code, and church. In 1867, Quebeckers held that Confederation gave Quebec rough parity with the rest of the country. French Canada, located largely but not solely in Quebec, was a force equal to English Canada. This is crucial to an understanding of modern-day Quebec's demands. The notion of Quebec not as an equal but as merely one province among ten, so deeply rooted in English Canada's current understanding of the country's structure, has always been unacceptable to Quebec.

As each new province was added to the country, Quebec's powers became diluted: policies that undermined francophone settlement in the West were developed; constitutional rules that might have protected francophone minorities were not enforced. The Quiet Revolution of the 1960s transformed Quebec into a modern industrial society and witnessed the growth of a renewed pride in Quebec's history and culture. A new secularism replaced the church as the focal point for French language and culture. The self-determination that emerged was a result of the constitutional imbalance that had developed in the years since Confederation.

The Right of the Collective

This emphasis on self-determination created a new perspective in Quebec — the concept of collective rights. This concept is quite different from the more common English notion of individual rights, which forms the basis of Canadian law and Canadian thinking on equality and human rights. Any answer to the current conflict between Canada and Quebec must recognize this difference and find a way to balance these fundamental approaches to the issues of language and self-determination.

"If the country is to survive, we must re-think the foundations of federalism," says the University of Ottawa's Donald Lenihan. "In English Canada this means, first and foremost, coming to terms with a legal concept that French Canadians and aboriginal peoples take for granted: collective rights."

Collective rights protect and promote the welfare of the community; at times these must supersede the rights of individuals. They recognize that people are part of a culture and a community and that their identity is a product of the language, traditions, and customs of a particular society. Just as individuals can be discriminated against, so, too, can communities and language or ethnic groups. Protection of the rights of the members of these communities must sometimes be vested in the group as a whole.

This sense of collective rights is now seen in Quebec as the way to define and protect an endangered language and culture. Says University of Western Ontario law professor and editor-in-chief of the *National Journal of Constitutional Law*, Errol Mendes, "The major goal of law and society requires the harmony of the individual and the community rather than the supremacy of one over the other."

Pierre Trudeau brought to the national stage a view of nationalism that was at odds with the philosophy of collective rights blossoming in Quebec during the Quiet Revolution years. Although the B.N.A. Act recognized what Professor Mendes calls the "search for consensus and compromise between collectivities," the Trudeau vision emphasized individual rights over collective rights. He articulated the classic liberal view understood best in English-speaking Canada and embodied in most of the major freedom-of-expression decisions of the Supreme Court of Canada. Trudeau maintained that only the individual can possess rights and that the law must entrench the primacy of the individual.

He created the Charter of Rights and Freedoms to enable citizens to "transcend the accidents of place and time, and partake in the essence of a universal Humanity. They are therefore not coercible by any ancestral tradition, being vassals neither to their race, nor their religion, nor to their condition of birth, nor to their collective history."

However, it is this very ancestral tradition that has been of such soul-searching importance to Quebeckers. The fear is that if the individual is not bound by language and race, both language and race may disappear. There is good cause for such a fear. From Confederation to the 1950s, Quebec's population as well as the francophone population of Canada represented about 30 percent of the total.

Since then both have declined to 25 percent. The Quebec birth rate is one of the lowest in the world. In twenty years, if Canada and Quebec maintain their current birth rates, Quebec's share of Canada's population will drop another 2 percent.

Surely, one might argue, the way to compensate for a falling birth rate is increased immigration. However, Quebec receives fewer immigrants and retains only about half as many per capita as the other provinces. Quebec's immigrants assimilate into francophone society at less than one-third the rate that immigrants assimilate to English in the other provinces. Francophones who leave Quebec are subject to excessively high levels of assimilation.

For Quebeckers, language is the crucial means of establishing and maintaining culture. The French language has given Quebec's dominant culture a distinct character and has proved to be an integral part of its nationalism. Quebec's historical approach to constitutional rights therefore has been driven by the need to secure the survival of the French language and the French culture in a continent overwhelmingly dominated by English.

Federal bilingualism policies are important for francophones living outside of Quebec and, with French-immersion programs, have helped sensitize a generation of English-speaking Canadians to the French fact in Canada. But, such policies do not address the collective rights to linguistic survival and security in Quebec and have done little to stop the assimilation of the French outside Quebec. The francophone population outside Quebec has continued to decline; more and more, the seat of French culture in North America is Quebec.

The siege mentality that has developed around the language issue can be explained in part by the marginal status of the French language in key areas of Quebec's economy. The 1972 Gendron Commission report on the use of French in the Quebec workplace found that the domain of the language was characterized by "inferior duties, small enterprises, low incomes and low levels of education." Although there has been a marked improvement in recent years in the control by francophones of the Quebec economy, the continuing use of English as the language of its higher echelons is still a concern.

In this context, it is easier to understand why there is such consensus among the Québécois on the legitimacy of mandatory language enforcement. The collective right of the Québécois to live and work in French is vital to the way Quebec asserts its identity. This is what Quebeckers mean by a "distinct society"; and the rejection by English-speaking Canada of the constitutional status of Quebec as distinct has understandably added to Quebec's fear of seeing the French language and culture disappear.

Bills 101 and 178
Much of the recent controversy in Canada over the language issue came to a head with the introduction of Quebec's language legislation, Bill 101. Outside Quebec, the landmark ruling of the Supreme Court of Canada striking down the commercial sign language provision of this law came to symbolize the Court's upholding of the fundamental right of free expression over collective language rights of the francophone majority in Quebec. The Quebec government's use of the "notwithstanding" provision of the Charter of Rights and Freedoms in Bill 178 to override the court's decision was seen in most parts of Canada as a fundamental disregard for the individual right of free expression and aided in bringing about the non-ratification of the Meech Lake Accord.

Errol Mendes has an important insight to add to the debate. "What has been lost in this tragic debacle ... is that the perspective within Quebec from the francophone majority and government is largely in agreement with the rest of Canada's perspective on the need to protect fundamental expression. The only disagreement is over what constitutes fundamental expression and under what circumstances non-fundamental expression can be limited or denied in the interests of a collective right to linguistic survival and security."

The essential Quebec position is that both the individual right of freedom of expression *and* the right of the collective to linguistic security and survival are fundamental rights and that what must be evaluated is the balance between them and the measures used to protect both. Priority can be given to the collective right only when there is overwhelming justification for doing so, such as when the existence of the collectivity is threatened. Moreover, priority may be given to the collective right only in cases when the individual right is limited only in a marginal way. The Quebec position was that the limits placed on business enterprises by this legislation were limits of commercial expression only, not of politics or ideology.

What was at stake was the right of the Québécois to survive as a people, with their own language, culture, and collective history. To permit bilingual signs would be to return to the old, no longer acceptable notion of "duality" in Quebec. For Quebeckers, the measure was justified in that it limited only freedom of commercial expression, not personal expression. Quebeckers would consider personal expression of the individual a "fundamental right." That is why Quebec leaders rejected the attempt by the Catholic School Board Commission of Montreal to impose the

French language on all students at recess and in the school halls.

Is there room for compromise and mutual understanding on these conflicting visions of rights? The answer must be "yes" if we are to survive as a nation.

As Lenihan points out, liberalism has great inner resources. Grounded in the belief in freedom, it transformed itself during the nineteenth century. Driven by concerns over exploitation of the working class, liberalism tempered freedom with a commitment to equality. This culminated in the ideal of freedom as self-realization. "Reformers saw liberalism as a profoundly humanistic doctrine aimed at providing the best possible chance for everyone to maximize her human potential. The concept of equal opportunity which emerged laid the foundations for the welfare state."

In order to accommodate different visions of equality, we will have to seek a fusion of individual and collective rights. This process has already begun in our courts. For example, Canadian courts have enforced the Hate Provisions of the Criminal Code in cases of incitement of hatred against identifiable minorities. (This could not happen in the United States, where the right of the individual is supreme.) And although the Charter has been used largely to uphold individual rights, it has within it the capacity to recognize collective rights. It also permits affirmative-action programs for specifically targeted groups.

For several years, using the Charter, the courts have been building towards a new understanding of the rights of groups. In 1989, the Supreme Court took what Christine Jefferson of the Women's Legal Education and Action Fund calls "a uniquely Canadian approach to equality rights" in the *Andrews* case. The case centred on an equality dispute involving a question of professional standards, the argument for which was based on a group definition of citizenship. Section 15 of the Charter was used for the first time to define group-based equality rights; the decision emphasized disadvantaged groups instead of individuals as the litmus test of equality.

Indeed, the Supreme Court decision on Bill 101 recognized the Quebec government's legitimate right to protect the *visage linguistique*, the French face, of Quebec. In fact, it is entirely possible that had Quebec argued the case under Section 15 of the Charter, it might have won.

Canadians will have to come to appreciate the importance of symbolism to both the francophone and aboriginal communities, and the value of group rights to minorities by entrenching collective rights in the Constitution. The Canada Clause with which we open this book would be an important first step.

The concept of collective rights is intimately linked with the assertion of national identity. There are those, who for sound historical reasons, fear nationalism in all its forms. They are rightly frightened by the extremes to which it has been taken, particularly in this century. Others, especially the corporate proponents of an international economy, oppose nation-building on the grounds that it interferes with the free flow of capital and prevents the creation of a single international climate for investment. That is to say, nationalism interferes with their exclusive right to profit.

Canadians have by and large avoided the extremes of nationalism and have historically shied away from chest-thumping patriotism. Today we are seeking ways to assert our sovereign right to self-determination in the face of a threat to our institutions and economy. More than ever, in the face of transnational corporate abuse, the democratic will of a people is understood to be paramount. At the same time, the meaning of nation and nationhood is being dissected and revised in light of new international realities and the urgent need for Canada to participate in the creation of international curbs on transnational corporations.

However, as Canadians reclaim our right to independent nationhood, we must be prepared to redefine its limits or large sectors of the population will be left out. We must redefine our concepts of sovereignty and nationhood in order to establish institutional relations among members of the three founding nations of Canada: aboriginal, French-, and English-speaking. To do so, we will need to reverse our one-dimensional definition of a single nation. Our survival and emancipation will depend on our ability to build on well-defined aboriginal, French-, and multicultural English-speaking national identities and to channel the creative energies of those parts into a cohesive entity called Canada.

Sovereignty Redefined

The French word *nation* is defined in *Petit Larousse* as a *grande communauté humaine*, one that possesses a common history, language, and culture. In French, a "nation" can be a cultural group. It does not necessarily denote a geographic entity, as does the English term, which the *Concise Oxford* defines as "congeries of people . . . inhabiting a territory bounded by defined limits."

Sovereignty is defined by *Petit Larousse* as the supremacy of the people and comes from a principle of French common law established after the French Revolution, whereby authority, once held by the king, is in the hands of the people. In English, again from the *Concise Oxford*, the word means "supreme, as power . . . supreme ruler, especially monarch."

Perhaps because of these different interpretations of the

meaning of the word, most English-speaking Canadians
have approached the concept of "sovereignty" with trep-
idation, hearing Quebec's needs as threats. If only we
could understand the valid, collective demands of Quebec
and aboriginal *nations*, we could start the healing of Canada. Such a process must be based on a new definition of
sovereignty as a means of including groups now alienated
from the majority. Native lawyer Jenny Jack explains that,
for native people, self-government accords will bring her
people into Confederation as, at last, they will be acknowl-
edged to be a nation negotiating with another nation.

Most native people firmly believe that their ancestors
never gave up their right to nationhood. The aboriginal
nations negotiated treaties with the early Europeans. The
treaties gave each group rights to the territory they shared,
but retained the sovereign identity of both. They were, in
fact, agreements to live as different nations in one state.

It is this model towards which native people are working. Says Assembly of First Nations chief Ovide Mercredi,
"Quebec wants more powers or it will leave. We don't say
that. We want more powers, and we want to be included
in Canada." Aboriginal people want to bargain nation to
nation. "We are a distinct society with inherent rights. . . .
What we're talking about is forcing the white politicians
of Canada to recognize that we're a distinct people, and to
make that a constitutional reality."

The crucial issues for Canada's aboriginal peoples include the settlement of legitimate land claims, self-government, and economic self-sufficiency. None of these is
possible under the paternalism of the Indian Act, which
institutionalizes dependency. Inclusion of the aboriginal
nation *as a nation* is an absolute requirement for successful
constitutional talks, as is a constitutional amendment for
self-government.

Canada as a Distinct Society

The term "distinct society" has come to represent the aspirations of Quebeckers to be recognized by English-speaking Canada as having language and culture rights unique to Quebec. It is clear that Quebec is distinct from the rest of Canada. But Canada, too, is distinct, *vis à vis* the United States. Long ago our ancestors chose to build a different kind of society on the northern half of the continent, and generations of Canadians have nurtured this society and its values.

The histories of Canada and the United States are very different. Because our country is so vast and geographically harsh, and because we had such a sparse population, mostly strung out along the U.S. border, we had to develop a distinct economic model of sharing for survival. We entrusted our government to develop a mix of public and private enterprise to provide affordable services. This distinct economy not only served to foster a different way of life in Canada but also prevented us from being absorbed into the United States. To have permitted the marketplace to dictate all economic decisions would have doomed the young country.

So we developed a railway, an airline, a national broadcasting system, and some of the finest social programs in the world. We also developed mechanisms to maintain some measure of economic control in the face of massive, American domination of our industry, resources, and culture. We created a constitutional requirement to provide equality of services to our regions and built a country based on survival, not domination. In this, we created a society sympathetic to the concept of collective rights.

Now it is urgent for us to take back this distinct heritage and build the future on a renewed understanding of its importance. It is imperative for Canadians outside of Quebec to know who we are and why we are fighting to preserve Canada. We will be able to be more generous and tolerant regarding the needs of Quebec and aboriginal peoples when we understand and value our own unique identity.

As Tony Clarke, chairperson of the Action Canada Network, says, "The historic struggle of aboriginal peoples and immigrant workers, plus the diverse cultural heritage of our regions will have to be woven into a new national vision. Those characteristics that have long distinguished Canada from the United States — such as greater emphasis on communal values, collective rights, environmental preservation, public enterprise —should be key elements in defining ourselves as a distinct society."

Options for Canada
There are, as we see it, three clear constitutional options for Canada. The status quo is not one of them. Quebec has told Canada that it must come up with an alternative within the year. Although support for sovereignty in Quebec has diminished somewhat, a lack of response from Canada would rightly be seen in Quebec as a rejection of its need to redefine our current system. The status quo is equally unacceptable to aboriginal people.

Nor would Meech Lake have provided a good alternative, as it represented a further weakening of our already shaky institutions. While there were and are bigots in Canada who used the accord to further their own ends, many other Canadians rejected Meech not because it gave special status to Quebec, but because it gave federal powers to the provinces, powers greedy provincial leaders were all too ready to grab. (Quebec had only five basic demands, but additional powers sought by the other provinces complicated the process and hastened its failure.) Had the accord been forced on these Canadians, given their anger at Quebec's high level of support for free trade, it might have added to an anti-Quebec backlash.

Moreover, the negotiating process of Meech Lake was the same process that has marred all constitutional negotiations in this country: the elite negotiated and set out to impose its will on the people for its own ends. Brian Mulroney behaved shamefully in telling Quebeckers that all anti-Meech sentiment was a rejection of Quebec and of francophones. He helped create a climate of anger and distrust on both sides at the very time he should, as prime minister, have been a peacemaker.

Now, we have a chance to change our Constitution in a way that will, finally, get it right. We must not waste this opportunity.

Option One: Decentralization — The Corporate Option

The provinces are likely to be offered — after another long "consultation" by Joe Clark — a constitutional "buffet" of federal powers including health care, communications, language, and Unemployment Insurance. The pot will be sweetened by a promise of Senate reform. Provinces will be allowed to opt in or out of social programs, with the likely result that richer, more powerful provinces will opt out, taking, as one does at all buffets, more than they can chew. The poorer provinces and regions will have no choice but to stay in; but there will not be enough money to support the programs once the major players have left the field.

The government and the BCNI will deny that the changes proposed by the corporate option represent decentralization. They will point as proof to the increased role of the federal government in key economic areas needed to strengthen our "competitive" edge. They will not mention that these increased federal responsibilities are being turned over to the private sector, and therefore will be of greatest benefit to the corporations.

Decentralization will be sold in Quebec as a recognition of its special status, as Quebec will be able to take most of the powers the Allaire Report asked for. In the rest of the country it will be billed as giving every province the options offered to Quebec: in essence, as not giving Quebec special status. This will not fool Quebeckers, whose bottom-line demand is recognition that it is a nation with the right to decide its own future. Powers given to all, not unique to Quebec, will not satisfy this demand. Even if the federal government enshrines the distinct society in the Constitution, it will not have any meaning if all that makes Quebec distinct is offered to everyone else as well.

The government will set out on a cross-Canada "consultation" to make Canadians believe that they are being heard. But their constitutional changes have been in the works for a very long time, devised by senior bureaucrats who have been given a full mandate for fundamental change. The Spicer Commission, no matter what its intention or the goodwill of the many hundreds who participated in the process, was a diversion. The real work was done away from the public eye.

Decentralization would be the worst possible option for Canada, already one of the most decentralized federations on earth. As long ago as 1979, an Economic Council of Canada report warned that Ottawa was "becoming increasingly powerless to the country as a whole and the welfare of Canadians." And this was before the dismantling of our energy and transportation systems and the slow strangulation of our social programs. Further devolution of federal powers will leave Canada without a centre, an international presence, or national cohesion.

Economists Richard Harris of Simon Fraser University and Douglas Purvis of Queen's warn that Canada faces a slow breakup if it abandons the concept of a strong national government. Giving the provinces more power will lead to tensions, interprovincial trade wars, and loss of mobility for individual Canadians. Says Harris, decentralization is designed to force Canada to adopt American thinking. "The end result of this sequence of events, which might play out over a decade or more, would be regionally based countries along the northern border of the United States which were economically and politically independent ... any defining characteristics of being a Canadian would a thing of the past." This would lead to "pressures from the U.S. for policy harmonization — a U.S.–defined level playing field."

Rejection of this option, however, is not an endorsement of the current system. There is a legitimate need for greater community control and decision making in the division of powers in Canada, whereby the administration of services could be far more locally based. But, it is essential to understand that the decentralization option is a vital part of the government's economic strategy for Canada. Continental trade and the gutting of the federal power structure are intricately linked. Like the GST, the made-in-Canada recession, and the high dollar, they are part of an agenda to force Canada through fundamental change. With them will go Canada's philosophy on the role of democracy and its sense of collective identity and rights.

It is essential also to understand that, just as power politics have formed the basis of past constitutional failures, they are alive and well today, in Canada and Quebec. The leaders of the Liberal, Parti Québécois, and Bloc Québécois parties in Quebec have all endorsed the Mulroney corporate agenda for Canada, an agenda that is devastating Quebec. For them, the most urgent problem is how to espouse Quebec nationalism without diluting the power of Quebec's corporate elite or giving up Quebec's ties with corporate Canada; for they are part of the continental trade block as surely as their counterparts in Canada and will do little to jeopardize these corporate interests.

The policies they back are being paid for by the citizens of Quebec. The manufacturing losses as companies flee to greener pastures are second only to Ontario's. In Montreal alone, the unemployment rate is almost 15 percent and youth unemployment stands at 25 percent — the highest level of any urban centre in Canada. One-quarter of Montrealers are living in poverty, the highest municipal rate in Canada. The Canadian Apparel Manufacturers' Institute expects the free-trade agreement to kill one-third of its 40,000 jobs in the Montreal region by the year 2000. Bankruptcies jumped by 50 percent in Quebec in the last year.

The decentralization option would be bad for the citizens of both Quebec and Canada. Although it will be sold as the only answer that will keep Quebec from leaving, it would, in fact, hasten the breakup of the country and destroy our social foundations. This option is a disastrous continuation of the historical manipulation of the people by the elite that has marred constitution-building in the past.

The people must say no.

Option Two: Separation

The second option, separation from Canada, is Quebec's to make, and Canada must accept Quebec's right to self-determination. That being said, it is far from clear that the majority of Quebeckers wish total separation from Canada. One poll, for example, found that a majority of Quebeckers prefer a form of renewed federalism to outright independence, but defined "renewed federalism" as a form of sovereignty. This poll and others suggest that, if Canada is prepared to alter the terms of Confederation, and recognize Quebec as a distinct *nation*, the majority of Quebeckers would opt for a continued and even revitalized relationship with Canada.

If Quebec does separate, the failure will be Canada's. It will mean that the rest of the country was unable to broaden its concepts of sovereignty and nationhood to accommodate Quebec's special needs. Understandably, many Canadians are tired of constitutional wrangling and ask in exasperation, "What *do* they want?" But it is urgent that we not give in to anger, frustration, or easy answers. "Let Quebec go" may be mere pique, but the consequences for Canada would be enormous.

Economists and others warn Quebec about the dire consequences to its economy should it separate. What must be understood, however, is that Quebeckers are prepared to suffer hardships in order to be masters in their own house and will sacrifice real income to maintain their culture. (Other Canadians, looking at the devastating effects of free trade on our culture and economy and wary of the ramifications of cancelling the deal, could take some lessons on backbone from Quebec.)

However, what the Quebec leadership has in mind for Quebec if it separates should give its citizens pause. Both the Liberals and the Parti Québécois have said they would negotiate a free-trade deal with the United States. Quebec has more nationalist practices and structures than other parts of Canada, built up over the years to protect Quebec industry and promote an indigenous economy. Government agencies such as the Caisse de dépôt and Hydro-Québec serve the needs of Quebeckers openly.

Said René Lévesque in 1968, "By nationalizing electric power, by creating the Société générale de financement du Québec [Quebec's industrial development bank] and the Caisse, we have taken the first steps toward the kind of collective control of certain essential services without which no human community can feel secure." In 1982, then Caisse chairman Jean Campeau said the corporation was "on the lookout for investments likely to strengthen the industrial structure of Quebec and bring in suitable returns." As well, Quebec has huge financial institutions such as the Mouvement Desjardins, which is based on a credit-union system of banking, and the Quebec Federation of Labour's Solidarity Fund, which lends exclusively to Quebec companies.

American business interests would never permit these and similar Quebec institutions once Quebec was negotiating as a separate country. International trade specialist Pierre Pettigrew says that Quebec does not operate according to the rules of American capitalism. In a free-trade deal, he asks, "How long will the United States accept an economic model which does not fit into its own philosophy?"

Simon Reisman, Canada's chief negotiator of the Canada-U.S. Free Trade Agreement, says that Quebec was at the heart of several problems the Americans wanted to resolve before they reached an agreement on the deal. He cited Hydro-Québec, the provincial liquor agency, and farm subsidies. "I know," says Reisman, "I was there."

Inclusion of a sovereign Quebec in the continental free trade process would put more than just these institutions at risk. Quebec would become more dependent on the United States for trade and for the survival of its economy. The American free-market, transnational-dominated agenda would have little time or patience for the collective cultural and language rights of Quebeckers. As free trade moves south, Spanish and Portuguese will become more prominent on the continent and French less so. Canada, no longer tied to Quebec, would not feel the same dedication to the survival of its culture, and Quebec might find itself very isolated. Quebec would become locked in to the U.S. orbit and would find it hard to return to an arrangement with Canada, if it so chose.

The agenda of both the Liberals and the Parti Québécois includes ploughing ahead with the James Bay project, although the latter is more sensitive to the rights of the Cree. Separation would likely speed up massive hydro exports to the United States, as Quebec's best chance for survival as an independent nation. A separate Quebec would likely find that putting its vast water reserves on the negotiating table would be a central precondition of a free-trade deal with the United States.

The truth is that Quebec's political leaders put pleasing U.S. business concerns ahead of the needs of Quebeckers. They flagrantly give preferential hydro rates to foreign-owned corporations through Hydro-Québec. Barbara Robson of the *Winnipeg Free Press* points out that a blue-chip committee struck by Robert Bourassa in 1986 sought advice on power sales to foreign customers from such U.S. presidential advisers as James Schlesinger, former U.S. energy secretary; William Simon, one-time U.S. treasury secretary; and Charles Curtis, former U.S. deputy secretary of energy — a man described by the powerful U.S. coal lobby as Washington's foremost power attorney.

Robson says that U.S. supporters of electricity imports from Canada saw the boon very clearly at the height of the debate on free trade. In 1988, a discussion paper produced by Harvard University's John F. Kennedy School of Government asked the question, "If the Canadian government wishes to consume their resources in order that U.S. householders can enjoy lower cost power, should the U.S. object?"

Chief among the new Hydro-Québec clients are U.S. utilities. The Harvard discussion paper estimates that U.S. utilities saved $283 million in 1986 alone by substituting $766 million worth of Canadian electricity for power they otherwise would have had to generate by burning U.S. coal or Middle East oil. In 1987, the Canadian National Energy Board ruled that utility tax exemptions and other indirect subsidies could not be passed on to U.S. customers. But, in 1990, amendments forced by the free-trade agreement stripped the NEB of its authority to rule on the pricing of exports. The people of Quebec are subsidizing American consumers, and an independent Quebec would be under considerable pressure to increase hydro exports.

An intensification of northern development to keep up with growing American demands will not be tolerated by the Cree of the area, who are fighting the next stage of James Bay. Any talk of Quebec sovereignty draws forth demands for sovereign control of the North by the Cree. As a sovereign nation in a hemispheric free-trade zone, Quebec would be under enormous pressure to lower its environmental standards in order to maintain economic prominence. As a result, ownership of the territory of the North would most surely be challenged by aboriginal peoples as part of their assertion of nationhood. "If there is no discussion [about sovereignty for the Cree], I can guarantee you that there will be violent confrontation," says Billy Diamond, the chief who negotiated James Bay I with the Bourassa government.

Dismayed by massive clearcutting of the northern forests in preparartion for the next series of dams, Diamond says that the government is vastly underestimating the Crees this time around. He adds, "Since Allaire, the issue is sovereignty . . . Quebec is going to discover it does not own two-thirds of its province."

Canada would be unalterably diminished by the loss of Quebec. Whatever tolerance we have developed — and it has been sorely tried in recent years — comes from the efforts of generations of ordinary Canadians to live in harmony, regardless of language or culture. Support for official bilingualism will not likely last when the francophone population of Canada — the current francophone population outside Quebec — totals 4 percent. The federal policy of bilingualism is at present well accepted in English-speaking Canada and its loss will be the loss of yet another foundation for tolerance. Overwhelmed by Ontario, divided geographically, and bitter as we will surely be after a protracted battle over land and money, Canada will struggle to survive in the new continental order.

Is there not a way for Canada and Quebec to solve these differences and get on with tackling the real problems that confront us both: poverty, environmental degradation, racism, growing violence, unemployment, and the continental corporate agenda that threatens the very existence of both Canada and Quebec?

Option Three: Nationhood Revisited

Richard Simeon, vice-chairman of the Ontario Law Reform Commission, points out that 89 percent of Canadians outside Quebec and 83 percent of Quebeckers agree that Canada is the best country in the world in which to live. Two-thirds of Quebeckers and four-fifths of those outside Quebec believe they have more in common with Canadians in other provinces than with Americans. Seventy-nine percent of Quebeckers and 89 percent of Canadians think it worthwhile to try to solve the national-unity problem. Huge majorities in both dispute the notion that Quebec and the rest of Canada don't have much in common.

In these statistics lies a vast common ground. Says Simeon, "Often what drives us apart is not the substance of policy, but symbols and the perceived structure of power." The failure of the Meech Lake Accord was perceived in Quebec as proof that Canada was not prepared to recognize the centrality of these symbols to Quebec, most particularly, the acknowledgment that Quebec is a distinct nation. Canadians want Quebeckers to respond to Canada in the same way they do; but this is simply not realistic, given the francophones' need to protect their culture and language first.

Alain Dubuc, editorial-page editor of *La Presse* in Montreal, explains that most French Quebeckers define themselves as Québécois first and then as French Canadians or Canadians. "This is the heart of the matter, more significant than any political option. It means that Quebeckers don't see Quebec as a province, but as their country, a perception so deep that it doesn't fluctuate with political events. It doesn't imply that all those who define themselves as Quebeckers will choose separation. It is perfectly possible to be Québécois and comfortable in

Confederation. . . . But it clearly means that they will not define their relationship towards Canada in the same way that other Canadians do." If Canadians can come to terms with this, we can live in harmony with Quebec.

Canadians who refuse to recognize this fundamental reality must stop and think. Are we ready to break up the country over this issue? Does it really affect the quality of life of someone living in Red Deer or Gander if the first allegiance of someone living in Trois-Rivières is to Quebec? Could we justify such a rationale to our children when they ask us how we let the country go? Is our pride so important that we will watch Quebeckers leave before we will open our hearts to the reality of their special relationship with Canada?

We need a new social contract based on the fundamental principle that the country of Canada is made up of three founding nations, each with inalienable rights to protect its sovereignty, historical roots, and culture. Any package that Canada sends to Quebec that does not recognize this principle will be rejected. Monique Simard, from the Confédération des syndicats nationaux, of Montreal, says, "Quebec must be able to decide unequivocally and definitely on its future. It must put an end to hesitations concerning jurisdictions and special status, and clearly indicate what it wants. It is time to admit once and for all that we must break this vicious circle and put an end to the eternal constitutional debate."

The third constitutional option would permit Quebec to define the level of autonomy it requires to feel safe and welcome in the Canada of the twenty-first century. It may very well be that Quebeckers would choose sovereign control only over culture and language. Those who fear for the rights of the anglophone minority in Quebec could rest easy if this option were chosen. For, as the anger over

Meech Lake fades, Quebeckers would be able to be more tolerant of anglophone concerns. A recent poll indicates that most Quebeckers would scrap Bill 178 if they could get an acceptable constitutional deal from Canada. And almost as many would favour an end to limits on English-language schooling if they felt adequately protected in the deal.

It may be that Quebeckers would choose to opt out of more programs and economic arrangements. Many Canadians will ask, "Why should Quebec have more power than the rest of us?" But opting out gives Quebec more *autonomy*, not more power. There would be consequences for Quebec, for by taking more responsibilities for itself, it loses proportional authority within the federal structure. Whatever the percentage of powers Quebec chooses to take over, transfer payments to Quebec would be cut by the same percentage; the responsibility for the corresponding taxes would be moved over to Quebec from the federal level as well. In areas in which Quebec would choose exclusive jurisdiction, it would lose the right to be involved at the federal cabinet level. The door would always be open for Quebec to re-enter these national programs and to be eligible for federal transfer payments that accompany these powers.

The people of Quebec should have the right to decide on the degree of autonomy they want, and some process should be established to give them more than an "in or out of Canada" option. If Canada could accept the third option, there is a greater possibility that Quebeckers would not choose to opt out of Confederation entirely. Although Quebeckers are more likely to opt for more autonomy than other Canadians, they are likely to demand fewer powers than their political leaders would seem to seek in the Allaire Report.

Only when the people have been consulted will we know if this new arrangement is workable politically. If Quebec assumes many new powers, then the current federal system may be unworkable. We will then be able to choose among a number of structural options, including the "two-parliament" option, rejected in the Pepin-Robarts Commission of the 1970s. In this set-up, one parliament would represent the nine English-speaking provinces, and a "national" parliament for all ten provinces would deal with areas of joint jurisdiction.

Many will say that this option opens the door to complicated political wrangling and complex new bureaucratic problems. That may be so. But, most assuredly, so will the process of separation. At least this option maintains the goal of working together to find a mutual solution.

The third option would not extend this autonomy to the other provinces. What the West, the North, and Atlantic Canada are seeking is more power at the centre of Confederation, not more autonomy. Recently, a reformed Senate has been seen, particularly in the West, as a means of gaining a greater voice at the national level of government.

To right the real and historic grievances of the regions, the Senate should be reformed along regional lines and the representation adjusted for balance. (For instance, before the latest Mulroney appointments, the Atlantic provinces were represented by thirty senators while the four western provinces combined had only twenty-four. This should be changed.)

The party in power in the Commons is usually not representative of all regions, and blocks of MPs from certain provinces can dominate the national agenda. As well, the prime minister and cabinet have, at present, far too much power; and the party discipline central to parliamentary behaviour allows the cabinet even more freedom. This means that regional interests that do not dovetail with the priorities of the executive are not likely to get a fair hearing, let alone serious consideration as the basis for national policies. A reformed Senate would help give regional interests the protection they do not get in our present parliamentary system.

Instead of representing provincial interests, as the federal-provincial conferences do, a reformed Senate would represent regional interests: Atlantic, Quebec, Ontario, Prairie, and Pacific. The North and aboriginal nations would also have to be formally recognized, perhaps as a non-geographic region with voting rights. Senators would be directly elected by the peoples they represent, on a proportionally represented basis, and would naturally run on regional issues. In this way, the anti-national forces of decentralization can be stopped while long-standing and legitimate regional interests are given formal recognition in the very structure of power.

The first step in this process is for Canada to offer to negotiate with Quebec and the aboriginal community, in two parallel processes. The offer should be based on the concept of three founding nations and the third option proposed here. A written commitment to be guided by these principles could be submitted.

Central to these talks, and probably most immediately controversial, would be the James Bay project. This is a very important test case for the new Canada. Quebec would see any involvement by Canada as interference. The Cree would demand federal support for their claim to sovereignty over the north of Quebec. This situation exposes a conflicting interpretation of the rights of self-determination. Quebec must understand that just as it views the project's successful completion as proof of its sovereign rights over its territory, the Cree and, indeed, the aboriginal people of Canada, see stopping it as their test of nationhood.

And just as Quebec is asking Canada to understand its need for self-determination, so too must Quebec understand and come to terms with the rights of the first peoples within its borders to the same. It would be the responsibility of the federal government in this case to negotiate a settlement on behalf of the Cree that protects their safety, livelihood, and environment.

The future of negotiations among Canada, Quebec, and the aboriginal community would be dependent on the successful resolution of this dispute. While the process would no doubt be painful, the possibility of finding a peaceful, fair solution is much greater if the three founding nations of Canada sit together, as nations, to negotiate than if a separate or separating Quebec, a non-sovereign native delegation, and the country of Canada attempt to do so.

Canada Renewed
The renewal of Canada must include the entrenchment in the Constitution of the right to aboriginal self-government, creating and recognizing a new order of government. The right of francophones outside Quebec to continued basic services in French is part of our historic obligation and must be honoured.

Fundamental also is our rich heritage of ethnic diversity; this heritage must be the centrepiece in the development of a concept of social rights that would be entrenched in the Constitution. Legal rights are protected in the Charter now, but the social rights of all Canadians to universal health care, pensions, and care for the young should be included in the Constitution to prevent future governments, captive to the interests of big business, to undermine or destroy them. Such an affirmation of social goals would serve not only to protect and strengthen our social structures but would help Canadians define ourselves and our responsibility to one another.

A renewed Canada must reaffirm a positive role for government. The temptation, after almost seven years of the Mulroney Conservatives and their destructive policies, is to write off politics and the political arena completely. This is the worst thing we could do. The need to become involved is more urgent than ever, as is the need to articulate a role for government that is different from the corporate definition currently being promoted. Unlike the United States, we have an historical expectation that government will work for the common good.

Finally, a renewed Canada needs to find a method of inclusion for its people in constitutional negotiations. Crucial to these talks is the representation that has been missing at all former constitutional talks, particularly that of women and ethnic minorities. The multicultural diversity of Canada and Quebec must be a fundamental component of all future constitutional negotiations. If the government refuses the growing call for a constituent assembly, the people of Canada will have to establish their own. Never again will we be left out of this process.

The solutions for Canada are fraught with dangers. But not to try would be unforgivable. Says Thomas Berger, "If people of differing languages, cultures, races, and religions can live together harmoniously within a great federal state, perhaps they may learn to live together harmoniously in the wider world. In Canada we have democratic institutions, the rule of law, an educated populace. If we can't find a way to live together, what peoples, what nations can?"

7.

ECONOMIC RENEWAL

"The potential and the capacity of Canadians to do great things in and for the world is there. It needs the political leadership to break the spell."

— Eric Kierans

SINCE THE BIRTH OF OUR NATION, WE HAVE fought to maintain our separateness from the American colossus, resisting the North-South continental pulls. Economically, these struggles have intensified in the last forty years. The challenge for nationalists has been to bring in policies to strengthen the national economy as a counterweight to North-South integration. The continentalists, led by the corporate sector, would like to see that integration proceed as quickly as possible. From the early 1970s to 1984, both nationalists and continentalists had their victories and defeats. Nationalists were frustrated that policies have been weak and change too slow. Continentalists were thwarted in their efforts to exorcize interventionist policies.

All the while, North-South trade flows have continued to grow faster than the economy and we have become more dependent on the U.S. market than on interprovincial trade. Fifteen years ago, Ontario's trade with the rest of Canada far exceeded that with the United States. Today Ontario's trade with the United States greatly exceeds trade with all other provinces combined. Quebec has experienced a similar if less dramatic shift.

The coming to power of the Mulroney government in 1984 represented a quantum change. As agent general for the corporations, it moved with great speed to dismantle the instruments of national economic control and to constitutionalize and sign a formal declaration of national surrender, the free-trade agreement. Lacking the consent of the Canadian people, the Conservatives did it by stealth, misleading Canadians about its significance.

To sell the trade deal during the 1988 federal election, they and their corporate friends had to promise that it would not hurt national sovereignty; that it would not hurt social and regional development programs; and that it would not hurt jobs and living standards. Indeed, they said it would strengthen the government's capacity to deliver these benefits. Discrediting their critics as liars and scaremongers, they presented themselves as champions of social consensus.

Once the trade deal was safely passed, however, they dropped the mantle of social champion with indecent haste and donned that of budget fighter and champion of competitiveness, confident that, once and for all, the continentalist tide was flooding the country.

In the corporate lexicon, "free trade," "competitiveness," and "decentralization" are merely flags of convenience used to mask the real goal — the accumulation of power and wealth. If the government of a country acts to restrict this goal, the corporate sector will minimize the hindrance through political influence or move elsewhere. Ultimately, it will seek to hijack the government, which then becomes its mouthpiece. This is what has happened in Canada with the ruling Conservative government.

We as a society must guard against any future Canadian government becoming so completely captive to the corporate agenda. For there is a huge chasm between corporate interests and the fundamental priorities and values of Canadian society. A democratic government that does not give precedence to the latter forfeits its legitimacy.

Transnational capital, because of its awesome productive power, is a dominant global political force. It will always be a major player in the Canadian economy and governments must negotiate with the transnationals to ensure that their productive capabilities are harnessed to bring benefits to Canadian society. As in any negotiating relationship, interests will, and should, conflict. Our goal is to ensure that the next Canadian government negotiates for Canada.

Cancel the Free-Trade Agreement
We believe, in light of the destruction caused by seven years of Conservative government, that the next Canadian government must launch a project of national reconstruction and development. Its first step in reclaiming national economic control must be to abrogate or cancel the Canada-U.S. Free Trade Agreement. Obviously, this means not participating in the current trilateral free-trade negotiations with Mexico, aimed at extending the core terms of the existing deal.

Legally this is a straightforward matter. There is a provision in the agreement (article 2106) which allows us or the United States to terminate the agreement simply by giving the other party six months' notice. Once we invoke the six-month solution, we would revert to conducting our trading relationship with the United States through the General Agreement on Tariffs and Trade (GATT). This is a multilateral arrangement involving some one hundred nations; both Canada and the United States have been a part of GATT for more than forty years. It provides a legal framework for conducting international trade that, though flawed, is far superior to the FTA.

There are two reasons why we have to scrap the free-trade agreement: one pragmatic and one symbolic. Pragmatically, we have no choice if we want to avoid eventual economic and political absorbtion into the United States. The costs of getting out — and there will be short-term costs — are far outweighed by the costs of staying in. The longer we're in, the more dependent we become, the higher the costs of getting out, and the more vulnerable we are to U.S. threats to cancel the deal unless we see things their way on "unfair" subsidies or other fundamental political choices.

Cancelling the deal also gives back to government policy instruments without which national development is impossible. It gives us back the ability to manage effectively our rich natural-resource base to ensure conservation and security of national supply. It enables us to encourage local processing of our resources, to stimulate the development of related industries, and thereby to diversify the economic base of many communities. It empowers us to price resources in a way that is advantageous to our own manufacturers. It allows us to consider water no longer a mere commercial good to be diverted to the United States.

Cancelling the FTA gives us back the capacity to set up new public-sector enterprises and/or restore, should we wish, those that have fallen to Tory privatization. It allows us to expand our national public health-care coverage to include a pharmaceutical and dental program. It allows provinces to proceed with public auto-insurance plans.

Cancelling the trade deal restores the power of our agricultural supply-management system to ensure that we are able to meet our national food needs. Food security, like energy security, is a critical element of national development. In Canada, careful management is the only way to compensate for our disadvantageous climate and geography.

The end of the FTA gives us back the ability to enforce the production safeguards of the Auto Pact. It allows us to insist that in this vital industry, the privilege of tariff-free access to the Canadian market is contingent on commitments to produce and create jobs in Canada. It gives government back the power to negotiate similar production-sharing arrangements in other sectors, to use access to our market as a tool of economic development.

It returns to us the capacity to regulate the behaviour of U.S. corporations in Canada to ensure their presence benefits the Canadian economy. It allows us to insist once again that they export, do research and development in Canada, use Canadian suppliers, enter into joint ventures with Canadian companies, issue shares to Canadians, and so forth. It permits us to increase Canadian ownership in key sectors, such as culture, oil, and gas, and to keep strategic high-technology industries — aerospace, telecommunications, biotechnology, etc. — under national control. It enables us to ensure that key areas, such as financial, health, and educational services, remain in Canadian hands. And it allows government to give incentives that favour Canadian-owned companies in designated sectors or regions.

Finally, cancelling the free-trade agreement gives us back the power to lower the Canadian-dollar exchange rate. The policy of the Canadian government to peg the dollar at 85 to 87 cents U.S. is accelerating the "restructuring" and harmonization of our economy. Regaining control of monetary policy will allow us to lower the dollar to the 70-to-75-cent range, thus immediately offsetting the enormous pressure we are under to harmonize our tax policies and our social, labour, and environmental standards to conform with those in the United States.

A 70-cent dollar would increase the price of imports (and certainly discourage cross-border shopping). It would increase the cost of servicing our foreign debt (but would dampen our appetite for further borrowing abroad). However, it would greatly improve the overall health of our economy. It would greatly expand production and employment in export industries and industries that compete with imports. Furthermore, a low interest rate that leads to an outflow of capital, and thereby a lower dollar, would further stimulate economic expansion.

To take back the enormous power surrendered under free trade is clearly a precondition of national reconstruction and development, but it will not be without consequence. The U.S. government and corporate interests in the United States and Canada may well retaliate.

This possibility brings us to the second, symbolic reason for abrogating the trade deal. The free-trade deal is jeopardizing our future as a nation. Thus, cancelling it is a symbol of our wish to assert Canadian sovereignty in accordance with international law, and that we want it, knowing that there may be retaliation. Canada must abrogate swiftly and directly. (Hesitation will only make worse the inevitable climate of political and economic instability.) However, if Canada acts strictly according to international law, the United States will be under greater

international political pressure to limit any negative response to legally sanctioned limits.

Canada is the United States' biggest export market,
accounting for one-fifth of its total exports. It will remain
so for the foreseeable future. It is, therefore, in the U.S.
interest to maintain stable economic relations with Canada. American producers may more aggressively use their
trade laws to harass Canadian exporters in certain sectors;
but they are aggressively using them now. (Free trade
gives little protection, as the steel and pork industries have
discovered.) Besides, they must conduct their trade actions
within the GATT framework.

The U.S. doesn't buy our products out of altruism. They
will continue to buy our oil, electricity, fish, softwood,
and minerals because it is good business and because they
need them. As well, much of our trade consists of parent/
subsidiary transfers within U.S. transnationals. This trade
has not been vulnerable to harassment actions in the past
and it is not likely to be in the future.

The corporate reaction to the Rae government in Ontario will give us a sense of what an abrogation-minded
government might expect.

The first budget brought in by the NDP goverment
contained very little new spending but, contrary to Conservative doctrine, held the line on existing programs,
despite the cutbacks in transfer payments.

"Economic disaster. Unconscionable," shouted the
manufacturers, who threatened to pull out their capital.
Conrad Black warned, "Capital and talented people will
avoid or flee Ontario until a more favourable climate
returns. . . . Ontario will pay dearly and long for its mind-
less submission to the NDP." The bond-rating agencies
jacked up Ontario's borrowing rate on the New York

financial markets. This is reminiscent of the reaction to the election of René Lévesque's P.Q. government in 1976. The present doomsday predictions will prove to have been just as exaggerated. Even with the resulting rise in the deficit, Ontario remains in a stronger financial position than the federal or many provincial governments.

However, the corporate elite does stand to lose its long-standing privilege from any government whose accession to power hasn't been bankrolled by the corporations. It will resist proposed reforms such as plant closure and labour legislation, pension-fund reform, taxation reforms, etc. Moreover, it will orchestrate a relentless media campaign to discredit reforms as unsound or irresponsible and thereby condition public opinion to a backlash.

One should not underestimate the power of big business to move its capital, especially in a Conservative-managed, free-trade environment. It is therefore important for an abrogation-minded government to maintain and build on the underlying strengths of the Canadian economy: a high-income market (the seventh largest in the world); an educated, healthy, and productive work-force; a good transportation/communications infrastructure; a rich resource and energy base. These, not whether the trade deal is abrogated, are the critical factors determining whether corporations stay and invest in Canada.

The election of an abrogation-minded government might cause short-term price and exchange-rate instability because international financial markets are unregulated and foreigners hold a high proportion of Canada's short-term debt. Thus, speculative capital outflows might frustrate a new government's efforts to manage exchange-rate policy. However, government has tools at its disposal, which are legal under international law, such as exchange and capital controls, to counteract these short-term effects.

As financial markets are most volatile in the face of uncertainty, it is essential that an abrogation-minded government be decisive and unambiguous about its intentions.

Mel Clark, Canada's former senior GATT negotiator, suggests that any risk associated with abrogating the free-trade agreement could be substantially reduced by taking four concrete steps:

1. Make termination a clear issue for the next election in order to win a mandate for abrogation. No democratic government could then challange it.

2. Conduct Canada's post-termination U.S. trade within the rights and obligations of the GATT contract by rigorously adhering to our obligations and consistently invoking our rights if the U.S. impairs them.

3. Expeditiously enact legislation which would prevent the corporate establishment from swaying party leaders, governments and elections.

4. Propose that both countries continue to eliminate all industrial tariffs except those relating to motor vehicles, and within GATT, propose that other industrialized countries do the same. If the U.S. refuses these proposals, Canada could move on its own.

Clark also warns against watering down this strategy with talk of renegotiating the free-trade deal, as has been proposed by Liberal leader, Jean Chrétien. This option fails to recognize that the FTA cedes very substantial power to the U.S. and that in bilateral negotiations, U.S. power greatly exceeds Canada's. "For these reasons, attempts to renegotiate the 'bad parts' would place Canada in a position similar to that of a country compelled to negotiate a peace treaty after losing a war, with a victor occupying all strategic ground on the frontier and directing harassing fire at the vanquished. Canada would be the supplicant trapped in a process controlled by the U.S., which would permit the U.S. either to demand and obtain additional onerous concessions or retain the status quo."

Several considerations would shape renegotiation talks to American advantage:

- The U.S. would begin such negotiations from the position that the FTA reflects a balance of rights and obligations and that payment must be made for any changes benefitting Canada;
- Since the U.S. market is ten times larger than Canada's, the U.S. would take the position that a symmetrical exchange of concessions relating to normal trade barriers such as countervailing duties would not provide reciprocity, and would demand additional concessions;
- Any conceivable FTA changes Canada would request would adversely affect powerful U.S. private-sector interests, who would oppose them;
- Any substantive change in the FTA would have to be approved by Congress, and there is a high risk that Canada would have to pay two or three times — first, to the Administration, second, the House of Representatives and third, the Senate.

Renegotiation of the deal is not a viable option, and talk of this possibility muddies the waters. What is called for is a clear and honest statement of intent to cancel the free-trade agreement and an open and democratic debate about this proposal in the country.

The call for abrogation can be a rallying point for Canadians to take back the nation, to reverse the corporate continentalist tide, and to begin a project of national reconstruction and development that truly matches the values and needs of our society. Given the severity of the crisis, it will require great strength of consensus and political will. We should remember that it took a war and the perception of an external threat to our society to pull us out of the 1930s Depression. It will take a similar national commitment to take back Canada from the internal threat.

Create a Fair-Trade Policy

Canada cannot and should not build walls around itself to shut out global realities. On the contrary, we need to recognize and confront two critical realities: transnational corporate power and our position in the shadow of the world's superpower. A strong and independent Canada is a necessary counterweight to these realities and would be a more useful participant in the international community than a satellite state slouching towards economic and political oblivion.

Being open to the world does not mean surrendering to the world. As tariff walls come down, as unregulated finance increasingly destabilizes national economies, and as the transnational corporations erode national sovereignty, it is all the more pressing that Canada adopt an interventionist stance. Historically, Canada has used high tariffs as a substitute for industrial policy. The galling irony of the free-trade deal is that it takes away these powers from us at the very time we most need them.

The free-traders' dream of an efficient, borderless world in which all of us are, somehow, better off is at best naively out of touch with the reality of power. At worst it is a myth the transnational corporate community spins to grab power from the nation-state. Free trade versus protectionism is a false issue; the real issue is who manages trade, and in whose interest. Should the corporations be given

free rein? Should the nation, the only potentially democratic expression of society's interests, have the ultimate
responsibility for managing trade?

During the last forty years, Canada has become increasingly dependent on trade, particularly with the
United States. Close to half our manufacturing production
is exported, and we continue to import more goods and
services than we export. More and more of our trade is
within transnational corporations, not open-market transactions. Our dependence on foreign capital continues to
grow: hardly any of our technology is homegrown; more
than half our manufacturing sector is foreign-owned.

"We have been overly generous to others who covet
our market and resources. We have catered to those Canadians who would sell our birthright to the highest bidder,"
says William Loewen, president of Winnipeg-based computer services company Comcheq Services Ltd. "We must
reverse the trends of the past forty years [and] give priority
to using our resources to produce goods within Canada.
We must embark on a long-range plan to raise the level of
Canadian ownership of all our businesses."

It is not to be assumed that trade is automatically good,
that more trade is better. We have to ask ourselves, is an
unselective export-oriented strategy in the best interests of
Canada? Is there a point at which export dependence hurts
our goals of national development? Trade policy must
always be an extension of national development policy,
not the other way around.

Clearly there are areas in which national priorities require that we limit trade. Preserving the capacity to meet
our national food needs and ensuring a secure supply of
energy and other vital resources are obvious reasons for
limiting trade. The need to build a strong technological
capacity in a given industry is another. Still others are

national ownership of our finance and manufacturing bases. Thus, we advocate a trade policy that might be termed "selective openness."

We as a nation have to build a solid foundation of productive industries that provide high-quality goods and services comparable to the best in the world and enable employment to be well remunerated. Our most precious asset is a healthy, educated, and prosperous citizenry. We cannot follow a competitive path that diminishes this most precious resource. Morally it is untenable; practically it is a dead end. Competition must take place within a social framework. Economic choices must ultimately be political choices. Political choices must ultimately be ethical choices.

Invest in National Development

A second step to taking back the nation is to secure and harness capital for national reconstruction and development. Frank Stronach's assertion that money is rootless and without allegiance need not be true. Through incentives and regulation, capital can become rooted in the national economy, shaped to fulfil national-development objectives.

Transnational corporations, Canadian and foreign owned, will be central to a national-development project. We can attract transnational capital and ensure a viable return. We have a high-income market, a skilled work-force, an efficient transportation/communication infrastructure, reliable energy supplies, etc. With the free-trade deal cancelled, we will also have the power to regulate corporate behaviour, to root it in the national economy, to require that it acts responsibly. However, regulations need not dissuade transnational corporations. In a negotiation between equals — a strong state and strong corporations — it is possible to work out a mutually advantageous *modus vivendi*.

There are also huge pools of national capital, the savings of our citizens, that can be harnessed for national development. For example, Canadian pension funds total $200 billion. Until recently only 10 percent of these funds could be invested outside the country. The Conservative government has raised that ceiling to 20 percent. We need to retrieve these valuable investment funds from the aimless pools of capital sloshing around the world so they can serve national-development priorities.

Quebec has been a leader in harnessing pension funds for public priorities. The Caisse de dépôts et placements is a $35-billion government-administered investment capital fund. It comprises the Quebec Pension Plan, major public-sector employee pension funds, the workers' compensation fund, and the Quebec auto-insurance plan. The largest single pool of investment capital in Canada, its mandate is to invest in Quebec-based industry. The Caisse is a major cause of the growth in the strength and confidence of Quebec business during the last decade.

Credit unions, democratic and rooted in communities, are another source of capital that can be mobilized for national development. The Van City Credit Union is a good example. With assets of $2 billion, it is the fifth-largest financial player in the Vancouver economy. Whatever happens to Vancouver, this capital is required by law to stay in Vancouver. Van City was the first Vancouver financial institution to provide small-business loans under $250,000; the first to grant women loans without requiring their husbands to co-sign. Its affirmative-action, wage, and benefit policies are having a positive effect throughout the industry. Its Ethical Growth Fund, which applies social and environmental criteria to its investment decisions, has been the top-performing mutual fund in Canada for the last three years, proof that applying social standards to investment can be profitable.

Co-op Atlantic is a network of co-operative businesses in Atlantic Canada owned by 170,000 families. It had sales of $1 billion last year and employed 5,000 people. Co-op Atlantic sells, retail and wholesale, everything from food and clothing to agricultural supplies; it holds one-fifth of the retail market in Atlantic Canada. It has credit unions and fishing co-ops. They are locally run and all the capital stays in the community. In a region that has suffered long from dependence and the outflow of capital, the co-op model offers enormous possibilities.

Success in mobilizing capital for development depends on establishing partnerships among governments, pension funds, private and co-operative businesses. A hypothetical example might be an employee buyout fund to help workers take ownership of their companies. The government sets up the fund, establishes the investment criteria, provides the initial capital, and acts as the guarantor. The pension fund buys bonds issued by the buyout fund and guaranteed by government. The fund buys the selected firm and places the shares in a holding company, in trust for the employees. Workers build up ownership paying back the fund through payroll deductions. Properly executed — preferably not as a last resort for a failing company — these arrangements can be an important development tool, providing stability for communities and a decent return for the pension fund and the new owners.

A central focus for a national project of reconstruction and development should be a special new pool of public investment capital. We could call it the "The Take Back the Nation Fund." Capitalized through long-term bond issues, it would appeal to Canadians as a way to respond to a national crisis in the same way they bought war bonds during the Second World War. The fund would provide long-term investment capital for projects reflecting national-development priorities: employment creation, environmental sensitivity, national economic control, productivity, etc. The fund would be divided into a number of subfunds or "windows," representing development target areas. They would include a community-development fund administered by community boards; a research-and-development fund providing long-term capital for Canadian high-tech companies; a Canadianization fund to help buy back vital industries; a farm debt-relief fund to help revitalize our agricultural sector; and a national-infrastructure fund to rebuild our decaying sewers and roads.

Create a Fair-Tax Policy

The third step in taking back the nation's economy is to right the imbalances in the tax system and restore financial integrity of government. Such measures will, first, hold the line and then gradually reduce the deficit, letting us, also gradually, restore the level and quality of our public services and allow us to reduce the size of the debt in relation to the overall economy. One thrust of these changes is to restore a measure of fairness to the tax system by cutting tax subsidies to the corporations and the wealthy, and by demanding of them a fair share of income taxes.

The previous Liberal government weakened the revenue-generating capacity of government in the mid-1970s by reducing the amount of tax they demanded from these two groups. Because government spending levels stayed the same, the result was a national deficit although deficits were supposed to emerge only in times of recession. When the recession did hit in 1982, the deficits accumulated from the good times made the post-recession debt much higher than it should have been.

The Tories then made things much worse. Not only did they continue to reduce taxes to the corporations and the rich but they drove up already high interest rates after 1987. Today one-third of all revenue goes to pay interest on the debt. Money is available for debt servicing because the government slashed programs and increased taxes, the most insidious of which is the GST, on middle- and lower-income groups. Irresponsible Tory policies have left us with a huge debt and severely deteriorated public services.

The Statistics Canada study discussed in chapter 3 leaves no doubt that the claim by business and the government that the current crisis has been caused by rampant social spending is irresponsible. (See page 86.) Through a campaign of misinformation, they have persuaded many Canadians that we have been spending beyond our means and we can no longer afford these lavish programs. In fact, it is the corporations who have imperiled the financial viability of the state. If corporate income taxes had grown at the same rate as personal income taxes (77 percent) and sales taxes (106 percent) since 1984, corporations would have contributed $9 billion more in taxes in 1990. If interest rates were five points below their 1990 levels, the federal deficit would have been lower by $8.5 billion according to finance department estimates.

The following actions, which would take back control and restore balance to our tax system and fiscal integrity to government, are broadly based on the work of Osgoode Hall Law School tax expert Neil Brooks:

1. Repeal the $100,000 capital-gains exemption (described in chapter 3). Take back $1.7 billion per year.
2. Repeal the tax subsidy on manufacturers' profits,

which reduces their taxable income. Take back $1 billion per year.

3. Repeal tax subsidies to real-estate developers that allow them to write off or depreciate the cost of their buildings even when they increase in value. Take back billions of dollars per year.

4. Repeal the business-meals and entertainment tax subsidy (described in chapter 3). Take back $1 billion per year.

5. Repeal the tax subsidy that allows transnational corporations to deduct costs of investments abroad and allows them to deduct interest on money they borrow to finance takeovers. This would reduce the export of jobs and wasteful economic activity. Take back billions of dollars per year.

6. Repeal the tax subsidies to businesses for expenses incurred in lobbying government. This would also reduce their political clout. Take back hundreds of millions of dollars per year.

7. Restore a progressive taxation system. The Tories lowered the top income-tax rate, which applies to the top 5 percent of taxpayers, to 29 percent. Restore it to 34 percent. Take back an extra $1.8 billion per year.

Add two new tax rates for the richest 2 percent of taxpayers (40 percent on income above $70,000, and 45 percent on income above $100,000). Take back another $1 billion per year.

8. Introduce a net-wealth tax. This would apply a 0.5 percent tax to the appreciation in the net worth (assets minus liabilities) of the richest 5 to 10 percent of individuals, allowing exemptions for such things as farms, owner-occupied houses, pension benefits, etc. Take back $1 billion per year.

9. Reintroduce a wealth-transfer tax. This would tax

transfers of property and other assets through gifts or death by the richest 5 to 10 percent of individuals. Take back $2 billion per year.

It takes an enormous amount of political will to do this. Rich individuals and the corporate community will bully and threaten to withdraw their money from the country. (Yet these are not wild-eyed proposals that would make Canada a pariah in the industrialized world. For example, most have a net-wealth tax; and Canada is the only country other than Australia that doesn't have a wealth-transfer tax.) Nevertheless, this is an essential step in taking back the national economy.

Draft a Canadian Social Charter

A fourth step to take back the nation in a project of national development is to entrench, in a charter, the social rights of citizenship that are an essential part of our collective identity. The inspiration for a Canadian social charter comes from the Europeans, who have established a social charter to shape the integration of Europe into a unified market.

The Europeans recognize that there is a social dimension to the integration process; that unless there is specific government action to prevent it, corporations will use their new-found mobility to force a competitive reduction of living standards among competing nations. The Europeans have, with the social charter, declared such competition "illegal." The guiding principle behind the charter is that the only acceptable competition is that which raises skills, productivity, and living standards towards the highest levels.

As Doris Anderson puts it, "Countries that look after people well, compete well. They strive for full employment and ensure that as many people as possible are well educated and trained for the work-force. The cost in the long run of not looking after people well — in crime, drug abuse, lost human potential, and a worsening economy — is too terrible to make any other solution a sensible alternative."

This is exactly the opposite of the Mulroney-Bush-Salinas approach in North America, which is designed to encourage companies to become competitive by depressing social and environmental standards to the lowest common denominator.

At present the European charter is at a very early stage, little more than a declaration of intent; the supranational legal structure has still to be put in place. However, the largest nations driving the European integration are among the most socially progressive and want to ensure that their standards are protected. This contrasts starkly with the North American situation, where the dominant partner is socially retrograde.

A social charter would not protect against the ills of the North American free-trade agreement, because none of the three governments is committed to the principles of social justice that would underlie it. On the contrary, a social charter would undermine the very reason for a free-trade deal. How could we trust the three negotiating parties to do anything other than legitimize the lowest standard? There has been talk of some kind of a social/environmental charter to "mollify" the opposition, as U.S. trade representative Carla Hills put it; but it can only be a hollow exercise and should not be encouraged.

However, the European charter could be adapted to the Canadian federation by a government of national development. (There is even a structure already in place to give it legal force subject to federal-provincial negotiation.) Setting up a social charter would send a strong signal that competition that sacrifices or compromises these rights would no longer be tolerated in Canada. It would force a fundamental shift in the way companies do business.

A Canada with a social charter would have to be protected from unfair trading practices known as social and ecological "dumping." This occurs when a company brings goods into the Canadian market from a country that engages in gross repression of labour and other human rights, or one that permits practices of gross environmental degradation. Canadian trade law would have to be amended to penalize imported products that gained their competitive edge in this way. This would prevent companies from putting undue pressure on unions to accept wage rollbacks and on governments to relax standards to preserve jobs. Our current trade law penalizes only companies that gain advantage through unfair pricing practices or unfair government subsidies.

A Canadian social charter might contain the following provisions:

1. full mobility of workers, including the removal of such barriers to movement as provincial professional requalification, lack of pension portability, etc.;
2. the right to adequate social benefits, such as health care, old-age security, unemployment insurance, etc.;
3. the right to earn a living at a decent wage, with a minimum , not a poverty wage, as it is now;
4. the right to join a union and bargain collectively, including the right to strike;
5. the right to a safe and healthy workplace;
6. the right to ongoing education and training;
7. the right to participate in consultations regarding

changes affecting the workplace, including technological change, takeovers, and closures.

A Role for Canada in the World

Canada needs to take back and expand its role as an independent voice in the international community. As a middle power, Canada has a stake in effective international
economic institutions that safeguard the sovereignty of
democratic nations and in international structures that
circumscribe the power of transnational corporations.

The International Monetary Fund (IMF), the World
Bank, and the General Agreement on Tariffs and Trade
(GATT) were set up after the Second World War in order
to avoid the horrors of the 1930s-style unregulated capitalism. They sought to ensure the orderly management of
economic relations among nations and to protect the ability of nations to pursue policies of growth, full employment, and income distribution. These goals, formally enshrined in their constitutions, have been subverted during
the past twenty years. The nations that control these institutions have converted them into global enforcers of an
economic order requiring that national priorities be subordinated to the free, unregulated flow of goods, services,
and capital, the very ills they were set up to prevent.

The people of the third world have borne the brunt of
these global inquisitors. Victims of financial crisis induced
by the northern industrialized nations and dependent on
the continued flow of northern financial resources, they
have been forced to adopt disastrous IMF/World Bank
structural-adjustment policies. These policies, which the
Canadian government ardently supports, have caused environmental degradation and increased inequalities between rich and poor nations and peoples. UNICEF
estimated in 1988 that the application of these policies has

been ultimately responsible for the deaths of one million children each year. The carnage has prompted one senior IMF official, Davidson Budhoo, to resign in order "to wash my hands of . . . the blood of millions of poor and starving people."

Virtually every indicator that measures the human condition has deteriorated in the lost decade of the 1980s, and some grisly perversities have emerged. Thanks to structural-adjustment policies, the third world is now a net exporter of food and capital — $50 billion per year — to the industrialized countries.

The structural-adjustment policies imposed voluntarily by the Mulroney government are inspired by IMF ideology and backed by the same corporate interests. The consequences for the Canadian population differ only in magnitude. Moreover, Canada's dangerously high international indebtedness could force a future government to go to the IMF for financial assistance and be forced to endure the same humiliating and destructive treatment as other debtors.

At the current round of multilateral trade negotiations at the GATT, Canada is supporting the U.S.-led effort to further erode national sovereignty by inserting into GATT many of the provisions achieved in the free-trade deal. If they get their way, the original purpose of GATT will be destroyed; instead it will become the global enforcer of transnational corporate rights and freedoms.

There is much that a future Canadian government could do on the international stage. Former disarmament ambassador Douglas Roche is calling for Canada to push for the U.N. institutions of common security: "a World Environment Agency with legal power to stop the grossest pollution; a U.N. Verification agency with the power to supervise mutual and balanced disarmament everywhere;

and a World Development Agency with the power to use world resources, such as mining the oceans and satellite technologies in space, for the benefit of all peoples, not just the already rich."

Canada could reactivate efforts to implement the U.N. Code of Conduct on Transnational Corporations, which the corporate lobby has succeeded in stalling for many years. It could advocate for a social charter as part of GATT, which would make trading nations that failed to meet minimum standards of human and labour rights liable to trade penalties. Canada could become a voice for sanity and fairness in the international financial community.

To take back our nation is inseparable from challenging the corporate tide world-wide. It is late in the day and the challenge is great but far from impossible. Popular democratic movements are everywhere asserting themselves.

Cuauthemoc Cárdenas, the son of one of Mexico's most revered presidents, is the foremost leader of the political opposition in Mexico. He has visited Canada three times since November 1990, meeting with political parties, labour, and other popular-sector groups. He is bringing a message that is dramatically different from what we have heard from the Mexican government. Cárdenas says that free trade is an unacceptable model of development for his country and an unacceptable way for Mexico to link itself with the United States, Canada, and the rest of the world. "Mexico will sell its cheap labour to attract foreign capital, which in turn will guarantee the survival of one of the last remaining authoritarian political systems in Latin America."

He believes people in all three countries will lose. He is reaching out to Canadians with a proposal for a different approach. "Our goal is to join forces with you and our friends, allies and counterparts in the United States, to build a just, sovereign and democratic continental relationship for the twenty-first century." Responding to the Cárdenas challenge is a good way to begin to take back the nation.

8.

THE RESTORATION OF RESPONSIBLE GOVERNMENT

"However stressful these times may be for Canada, we must not squander our national dream. Though at times it may appear unattainable, we are a stronger people for having it. Herein lies our strength."

— Marjorie M. Bowker

THE CRISIS THAT CANADA IS EXPERIENCING is a positive development. Canadians have been too complacent. We have taken democracy for granted and have not accepted personal responsibility for its survival. Sleepwalking towards extinction, we have surrendered the decisions on our political lives to self-interested elites. We have abdicated our collective role as protector of our institutions, economy, and future. Our history has been one of trust in authority, and that authority has betrayed us. Now we must overcome the political illiteracy that is the legacy of our apathy. Otherwise, our country will surely disappear.

Our behaviour, however foolish, is not a death wish, and extinction is not inevitable. Out of our ignorance can — and must — come knowledge. Out of our apathy, action. Out of our youth, maturity. The depoliticized Canadian people must reclaim our country. We must take back our nation, our nations, from those with no respect for our traditions and our needs, and no commitment to our future. If we do not set Canada on a new course, we will be contributing to social and economic unrest the likes of which our country has never experienced.

In setting this new course, however, we must build on hope, not fear. Canadians must say yes to future challenges, not just no to past mistakes. It will take enormous political courage to do what has to be done to forge a new reality, but in the process, we will create a society that reflects the best in us and is ours to govern.

Instead of reacting to an externally imposed agenda, we will have to define our own national goals and dreams and build economic and social policies on these aspirations. What kind of Canada do we want? What values bind us? What international reputation do we want? Will we serve the needs of humanity or the goals of the corporate conquistadors?

We are just two years away from the most critical general election in Canadian history: the nation-state of Canada will be on the line. Today, there is no clearly developed political leadership or strategy for opposing the corporate agenda. What is urgently needed is political leadership and action that reaches out to Canadians of all backgrounds to enable us to develop an alternative agenda for Canada's political future.

We have offered our political and economic alternatives for Canada in this book. What follow are the five concrete steps we believe Canadians must take to restore our nation. Every individual can make a difference. The process starts with an individual commitment to become involved. A clear understanding of the nature of the fight we are in is necessary. Then people can join community, provincial, national, and even international groups fighting the corporate agenda or challenge groups in which they are already involved to join the fight.

It is vital that Canadians know there is an active movement developing a strategic plan of action to take back the nation and create economic and political alternatives to the current agenda. Each one of us can become part of it.

Step One: Name the Issue

This step includes clarifying the issues at stake, choosing personal priorities to work on, and making the link between these priorities and the overall agenda.

First, we need to build an analysis that encompasses the urgency and scope of the crisis facing us. Most Canadians are experiencing part of the crisis. Families are trying to cope with job layoffs. Small businesses are retrenching to survive. Farmers are juggling to save their farms from foreclosure. Many communities are fighting the shutdown of their post office, rail or air service, or their CBC stations. Food banks are coming up short, crushed under the burden of need. Truckers, unable to compete with huge American carriers, are going out of business. Stores and gas stations are closing.

Most people, however, are isolated in their problems; all the groups and people affected can "explain" their specific situations.

But these situations are not unconnected. Canada is undergoing a fundamental restructuring. It is being transformed into the type of free-market economy advocated by the International Monetary Fund. We are witnessing the systematic and deliberate destruction of the nation we have known. The Canada that will emerge, unless we take action, will be a mere vehicle for the needs and wishes of the large corporate powers of the continent. Therefore, central to our analysis must be an understanding of how much power the corporate sector, both Canadian and American, holds in influencing the political agenda.

To achieve such control, the corporate power brokers have set out to discredit the importance of the political arena and the role of government to the national interest. All Canada needs, according to them, is the advice of their economists and technocrats to transform itself to a world-class, "competitive" player. Key to taking back the nation, then, is circumscribing corporate power over this and any other government. It is the interests of big business that have stolen Canada. It is from big-business interests that we must take it back.

The Canadian government is being transformed to serve corporate needs and wishes, by providing optimum conditions for their economic health: the free flow of money and manufacturing, no matter what the cost to Canadian workers; the most profitable opportunities for investment, no matter how many Canadian companies are thereby forced to shut down. All government economic decisions are being dictated by whether they enable these companies to become or remain competitive. The federal government will enable this to happen and divest itself of responsibilities that present impediments to this end. Such impediments include environmental stewardship, energy security, social programs, and the delivery of public services.

Our public institutions have been more than vehicles delivering fair distribution. Without them, Canada could not have survived as a nation. Only through these public enterprises did Canada develop our own industry, technology, transportation, and communications services. Massive abrogation of federal responsibilities will result, among other things, in an erosion of the public service and the resulting decline of Canadian enterprises and institutions.

If Canadians accept this larger analysis of the problem, it will help direct our actions. To lobby the government that is delivering the country over to the corporate agenda is obviously a waste of time. (To attempt to halt the cuts to the CBC, for example, while a noble and important gesture, is pointless, as the CBC in its current form is targeted by the government.) But understanding the scope of the corporate agenda and the many ways the government is facilitating it will help us focus on defeating this government and replacing it with an alternative that shares our concerns. It might also be used to combat emerging political movements based on the politics of fear and bigotry.

Moreover, most Canadians subscribe to the values of diversity, sharing, tolerance, and equality embodied in our social and cultural institutions. By understanding the fundamental attack on both the institutions and the underlying values they represent, we can bring to bear Canadians' strong sense of right and wrong. We have an upset, motivated, and impassioned population that will be best served by a coherent and comprehensive analysis of the nature of our crisis and a clear set of actions in which they can participate.

Practically, Canadians wanting to get involved can do so by setting priorities and choosing issues that matter personally to them. Some will be concerned about the threat to Medicare, others about education, fair taxes, or culture. Many will be involved with organizations currently working on these issues. By choosing to act in the context of an issue that is personally relevant, people can enter the process without feeling overwhelmed by the magnitude of the job to be done.

After reading the analysis chapters of this book, readers can relate to the larger agenda: "What issues really matter to me? How do my issues relate to the overall analysis here?" The danger is that we will all busily work, lobby, and write letters in our separate sectors, fighting our own small battles as the war is lost. The challenge is to understand the relation between the agenda of the transnational corporations and the individual areas in which we are working. It is essential that we then connect our individual issues to the larger agenda and work with others doing the same.

Step Two: Take Community Control

The next step is to understand how this agenda is affecting communities and to take back community control. The helplessness that Canadians are feeling regarding national politics is manifested in the experiences of our daily lives. Reasserting our democratic rights nationally begins with asserting them locally. Just as Canada has to rebuild an independent economy, so too must the communities of Canada participate in that rebuilding by establishing more control over their futures.

Local communities must begin to seek answers to long-standing grievances about who has authority over their lives and who controls the decision making. The economic solutions for Canada will involve increasing local and regional power in Ottawa. The process must begin now.

There are many communities in Canada taking the brunt of the new continental order. Winnipeg has seen its unemployment rate rise 50 percent in two years. The city has lost its meat-packing and textile industries and its retail sector is shutting down. As the East-West axis in Canada re-aligns to a North American North-South axis, Winnipeg is losing its place as a Canadian railway hub. CP Rail has been rerouting potash around Manitoba to U.S. markets. The loss to the province will exceed two hundred trains a year.

Says Frances Russell, "This city is dying. We have lost our whole *raison d'être* to free trade. What is there here except the East-West hub? When that goes, and our manufacturing goes, what's left?"

La Gaspésie, in Quebec, is facing social and economic erosion that threatens its very future. Individuals' income is 30 percent lower than the Quebec average, and the unemployment rate is twice as high. There is a continuing out-migration of the young, and a continual erosion of the agricultural sector and of community life. Fish stocks are badly depleted and the local CBC and ferry services have been shut down.

But in both these communities, people are fighting back. In Winnipeg, a group called Choices has been launched. Choices started when a handful of Winnipeg inner-city activists — who, one member explains, range from "left-wingers to Red Tories" — got together in 1990 to discuss how to deal with cutbacks to provincial services. It has grown into a potent political force in the city and has taken on issues from the provincial budget cuts to the school board. It is credited with saving the jobs of 1,000 Winnipeg civic workers.

Choices uses strong symbolism in its work, taking on projects that directly affect people's lives and finding relevant ways to publicize their issues. It picketed the Canadian Imperial Bank of Commerce, for example, to publicize the fact that libraries and swimming pools were going to be closed because big corporations such as the CIBC hadn't had a business-tax increase in seventeen years. Success is key to the group. Says organizer Jim Silver, "It's very important to build victory into the process. You can only take so many losses until your heart gives up. So Choices is taking on local issues — and is winning them. The right political decision, to start locally, was made and now people are getting ready to tackle more national and international problems."

He points out that a huge organization is not necessary as long as there is commitment, good planning, and research. "People want to express themselves politically. We need to find ways to help them to do that. The beauty of Choices is that you and I and others like us can become directly involved and do something."

Bertrand Blanchet, the Bishop of Gaspésie, is passionate in his belief that the people of the area have to take charge. He circulated a questionnaire in 1990 to all the residents, asking for their ideas and seeking their commitment to reverse the destruction of their community. The response was overwhelming. The residents laid a great deal of blame on federal and provincial policies that put the interests of big business before the needs of the people; but they decided to create a new future for themselves. They are forming local bodies to take control of the management of natural resources of the area, especially the forests, fisheries, and agriculture. Only the people can be responsible for the sustainable management of the earth's bounty, they maintain, and only they can establish practices that will serve future generations well. They are also developing secondary industry from these resources, controlled by local workers.

The region, including the local aboriginal community, is undergoing a rich cultural rebirth. The people of Gaspésie are building a strong tourism industry, based on a shared experience of the most precious commodity in our modern world: a land loved and cared for by a people committed to its preservation. The Gaspésiens are adamant that they be heard by their elected officials, that local and provincial institutions be made more accountable to them, and that their schools and churches reflect the people's new-found power. Says Blanchet, "The pessimists are right. But only the optimists change the world."

The truckers of southern Ontario are fighting the erosion of their industry and their communities as well. A diverse and independent band of individuals, the truckers have put aside historical differences and rivalries to create a new organization called Truckers for Canada. They have fought through political differences to reach a common analysis of their problems, which they describe as, "deregulation, the GST, and an unfair trade agreement." They have joined a coalition of groups fighting the same agenda and have developed a political strategy that includes tying red and white ribbons of protest and hope on their trucks and blocking Tory conventions and Parliament Hill.

Says Windsor trucker Wayne Whitney, "My own trucking company moved to the United States. They still have a place in Oshawa but they moved all our jobs. Now American drivers have our jobs and we have to sit outside and beg for a dollar. There is no hope unless the people stand up. I'm a truck driver, but I'm a Canadian first. I've paid a price for being Canadian, and I have a promise for Brian Mulroney: you brought the fight to our door step. We'll bring it to yours."

These are only three examples of local action that is building across the country. In developing a strategy to defeat the Mulroney government and the corporate agenda, we must build on these and other local initiatives. As people name the issues that matter to them and become politically involved in forging change, they will be more able to prepare for the next stage of action — taking on the national agenda. In taking back community control, Canadians begin to take back the nation.

Step Three: Join the Movement
This step consists of becoming personally involved in the local, provincial, national, or international movements to stop the corporate agenda. It requires individual commitment to action, finding the people and groups working at the different levels, and joining the fight.

There are two ways to view power and how to influence those who possess it. One view holds that society is organized in a pyramid. There is a powerful elite, at the top, supported by a large but relatively unempowered populace. Those in power control institutions, laws, traditions, and education; by means of this control, they serve their own interests. As the majority of people are powerless, social change can be achieved only by appealing to those in power through the institutions they control.

The other view holds that power ultimately resides in the population, and that those in power are there only with the permission of the people. (Even dictatorships are dependent on the co-operation, support, or acquiescence of the public.) How change is tackled in a society very much depends on which of these two views the people in that society hold.

We believe that Canadians can control their government and that, during the next two years, the Canadian public can be mobilized, through public action, to oust the Mulroney government and replace it with one that has the courage to abrogate the free-trade agreement and start Canada on a new course of economic and social reform.

The process has begun. There is a thirst for involvement by Canadian citizens all over the country. It can be seen in the sense of co-operation building in communities across Canada as a response to the harsh reality of the Mulroney agenda. New coalitions are forming to fight the corporate agenda and create a political space for the concerns and values of the people of Canada. A fierce determination to reassert political and economic sovereignty is developing from coast to coast.

Each person must take personal responsibility to stop the erosion of the country. As individuals, people can join the citizens' movement or encourage local groups to which they belong to take action. There are two principal vehicles for this action.

The Council of Canadians is a non-profit, non-partisan national organization devoted to the enhancement and preservation of Canadian sovereignty and political independence in economic, cultural, social, resource, and foreign policy. It was founded in 1985 by Canadian nationalist, publisher, and writer, Mel Hurtig and others to fight the free-trade agreement. The council was a leader in the fight against the deal, organizing demonstrations, lobbying politicians, and making the connections between free trade and the erosion of our sovereignty and our economic independence. After the 1988 election, the Council of Canadians vowed to monitor and fight the free-trade agreement and the government's other destructive policies.

Headquartered in Ottawa, it has grown to 21,000 members and has active chapters in most communities across Canada. The council has been on the front lines in the fight against foreign takeovers of Canadian industry and became intensely involved in trying to stop the takeover of Connaught BioSciences and Consumers Gas, among others. It fought the stripping of political power of the National Energy Board and the subsequent loss of control over our energy supplies. It was a founding member of a coalition to halt the gutting of the CBC and works with the cultural community to preserve its place in Canadian society. It is taking a leading role in proposing to Canadians the constitutional options presented in this book and has undertaken an extensive analysis of the views of its members regarding the Canada-Quebec question.

Canadians interested in working with the council can join thousands of people committed to building the citizen's network that needs to be in place for the next election.

The other organization is the most powerful coalition of people's groups ever formed in this country. Called Action Canada Network, it was founded at a Council of Canadians meeting held on the day of the third Mulroney-Reagan "Shamrock Summit" in 1987. It is made up of forty major national organizations representing labour, women, farmers, churches, environmentalists, teachers, students, nurses, seniors, native peoples, the arts community, international agencies, and anti-poverty groups, plus coalitions from every province. Its original purpose was to create joint strategies for organizations fighting the free-trade agreement and its accompanying agenda; but, like the Council of Canadians, Action Canada Network has matured into a permanent organization to represent the concerns of its member groups.

Commmitted to fighting the Conservative corporate agenda, the ACN has provided leadership in the fight against the GST, the gutting of federal transfer payments, and the destruction of national institutions. Canada's social programs, such as Medicare, are priorities and the ACN puts out an alternative to each government budget. It is taking the leading role in preparing a set of policies that is an alternative to the corporate agenda in preparation for the next election.

Canadians who belong to groups — church, campus, community, farm, or others — or are involved in provincial or national organizations whose mandate is affected by the corporate agenda can become involved in the Action Canada Network, at the national or provincial level.

As well, a continental alternative is being built. Under the umbrella of the Action Canada Network and in concert with Common Frontiers, a Toronto-based organization committed to fighting continental free trade, a three-country coalition has been formed to construct alternative trade proposals for North America. Groups from Canada, the United States, and Mexico have been meeting to design a mechanism for monitoring the talks, establishing ways of working together to defeat this agenda, and building the alternative.

Farm organizations in the three countries, for example, are sharing information on how transnational agribusiness has thrown millions off the land in many third-world countries, destroyed family farms in the United States, and is moving into Canada, forcing the end of marketing boards and dictating government policy. Canadian and U.S. auto workers are banding together to publicize and redress abuses to their counterparts in Mexico. The purpose of gathering and exchanging information is so that it can be presented to the public in the three countries to educate and enable them to fight back.

This coalition building should not be confined, however, to national organizations. As the world moves towards a global economy, it is imperative that the peoples of the world find common ground on which to establish their needs and rights. Canada cannot fight this transnational corporate agenda alone. Canadians must reach out to people and groups being affected in other countries and build opposition together. Church and other groups can "twin" with equivalent groups in Mexico. Environmental groups concerned, for instance, with toxic-waste dumping can work with groups in the United States and Mexico to monitor and expose environmental crimes being committed there. Women abused in the Mexican *maquiladora* need the support of North American women's organizations.

As the free-trade agenda moves farther south, these coalitions will have to be extended to affected countries. A positive outcome for the people of Central and South America could be the direct contact with more people in Canada and the United States, forging alliances against human-rights abuses and political persecution. North Americans will have a harder time ignoring the street children of Brazil and the disappearances of political opponents in El Salvador should our economies become intertwined.

This is a crucial moment in Canada's political history. It is essential not to become discouraged. We can see our future as an opportunity or as a danger, as a gift of renewal or a hopeless loss. It would be easy to feel a sense of despair as Canadians come to understand the overwhelming power of the transnational corporations and the difficulty of winning back the country. A sense of helplessness is furthered by the government,which has a conscious strategy to prevent its real agenda from becoming public. Rather than fostering an informed populace, the Mulroney Conservatives have attempted to keep us ignorant, believing an ignorant public to be easy to manage.

Massive public education is key to success at this point, and working to build as large a base of support as possible is critical. We must put out clear and honest alternatives, ones that encompass the long struggle Canadians have ahead to reclaim our country. People will accept their old world-view until presented with a new one, and that can come only through education.

And our alternatives cannot be built as long as there is exclusion. The new order excludes the plurality of the real Canada. A successful alternative must give voice to the voiceless, power to the powerless, and political literacy to all. Politics must never again become the fiefdom of an elite.

Step Four: Develop the Platform

This step involves creating the political and economic alternatives at community, provincial, and national levels; developing the platform of action; and building strategies for implementation. It is crucial that citizens have a platform for action on key issues. Our responses cannot be simply a negative reaction to what we don't want. We must be able to articulate what we do want. To rebuild our nation on hope and not fear requires alternative policies and models for political renewal.

The options offered in this book can be a starting-point. We are advocating a constitutional solution based on: the acceptance of three founding nations in Canada; affirmation of collective rights; the recognition and celebration of the distinct natures of Quebec and the first peoples; the recognition and celebration of Canada as a distinct society in North America; a reformed Senate to give the regions more power; recognition of the centrality of ethnic diversity in Canada; and a reaffirmation of an effective and progressive role for government.

To promote this vision, we are advocating a program of cultural renewal reflecting the above principles. It is through our artists, writers, musicians, poets, and film-makers that this renewal will be acclaimed.

Our economic options include: the cancelling of the free-trade agreement; a new trade policy based on "selective openness" instead of economic surrender; financing, through a reconstruction fund, national economic development, and independence; the restoration, through tax reform, of the financial integrity of government; and the creation of a Canadian social charter.

These can become the basis of our national alternatives and platform for action. For instance, if the federal government refuses to establish a constituent assembly, the member groups of the Action Canada Network working with the chapters of the Council of Canadians could undertake this project on behalf of the people of Canada. Regional assemblies could be created in order to give an in-depth voice to all regions.

Similarly, at provincial and community levels, the principles advocated here can form the basis for action. In concert with the national level, selected communities can become the focal point for direct action, with public events designed to dramatize the nature of the crisis in Canada as it relates to that community. Local groups can produce their own social charters and economic models to serve as prototypes across the country. The alternatives we choose must not come only from the national to the local level. Local communities must play an integral part in laying the foundation for the workings of a future Confederation.

In addition, we propose three specific areas of action for our platform to take back the nation.

Shop in Canada, Buy Canadian-Made Products
Canadian retailers are losing money and Canadians are losing vital jobs as friends and neighbours drive to the United States to shop. It is entirely understandable that Canadians suffering from a recession and high unemployment seek out lowest consumer prices. It is particularly understandable, given that the Mulroney government tells Canadians they don't have to think in terms of their country any more, but are part of the new continental market-place. However, we need to think about the consequences of these actions. Prices are, indeed, higher in Canada. This is partly because we are a small, mixed-market economy that can compete head to head with the giant assembly line to the south only if we merge our economy with that of the United States.

As Canadians lose jobs to cross-border shopping and free trade, the need for our social safety net is increased. Governments, without the revenues from lost jobs and consumer spending, are forced to choose between maintaining social programs or not increasing the deficit. Governments refusing to increase the deficit and abandoning their commitments to those in need condemn larger and larger numbers of Canadians to permanent poverty. Governments refusing to abandon the thousands of unemployed and their families will have to be willing to go into debt to fulfil this commitment. This produces a terrible double bind for provincial governments. If Canadians want to relieve the burden of taxes and debt, we must support other Canadians in their desire to work and contribute to the economy. This can be accomplished by implementing the economic alternatives we have proposed and by shopping in Canada, buying goods produced in Canada, and encouraging others to do the same. Buying Canadian saves jobs.

In time, as we rebuild our industry and economy, our prices will become more competitive. Meanwhile, short-term cheaper U.S. prices are costing us all dearly, in store closures, lost jobs, and growing breadlines. We need to rediscover the oldest of our Canadian values: sharing to ensure the survival of all.

Build Provincial Support
An immediate action Canadians across the country can take is to become involved in provincial politics. Several provinces are in the process of elections and we need to ensure that the issues that concern us at a national level are being addressed at the provincial level. Governments that support the Mulroney agenda must be defeated. Opposition parties that refuse to take a clear position on trilateral free trade, decentralization, and privatization must be challenged. It is not good enough for opposition parties to keep their heads down and skulk to victory on a vote against the current government. The very existence of the country is at stake and those running for provincial office must take a clear stand.

In Ontario, the former Peterson government passed legislation that gave the province jurisdictional rights over health, water, and energy — areas that might, one day, be challenged under the free-trade agreement. This legislation is a prototype that could be adopted by other provinces. The current Ontario government has promised public auto insurance, which also could be challenged under the free-trade agreement. (American private insurers would likely seek compensation for potential lost revenues. The prime minister would have to side with a private U.S. industry association over the elected representatives of the people of Ontario.) Bob Rae, the premier, has been steadfast in his criticism of the effects of free trade on the manufacturing sector of the province. Other premiers must be asked to do the same. If they refuse to respond to their electorates, they must be voted out of office.

Like-minded provincial governments — the current governments of Ontario and Prince Edward Island along with possible new governments in British Columbia and Saskatchewan — could form a block against the Mulroney government's policies and together fight its decentralization package. They could work together to develop, for instance, tactics to stall the subsidy negotiations in the trilateral trade talks with Mexico and the United States.

Citizens of these provinces could organize through the Council of Canadians, the Action Canada Network, or by becoming active in political parties, to encourage a strategy to stall the federal agenda until the Mulroney government is defeated.

Prepare an Anti-Decentralization Strategy
Many provincial political leaders will grab all they can in the federal-power giveaway the Tories will offer. Although Canada has real, and oftentimes painful, regional tensions, regional discord has sometimes been created by provincial powerholders anxious to boost their local support. Ottawa bashing is an old Canadian sport. The irony is that premiers who support decentralization in order to gain more power provincially will lose national stature, as opting out of a program will bar them from national decision making in that area. They will appear to be bigger fish but only because of the smaller pond.

The people of Canada, however, care very much about our country as a whole, and we are far less likely than our leaders to be tempted by the decentralization buffet. No provincial politician, with the possible exception of Robert Bourassa, was elected to lead a province out of

Confederation. Although we are opposed to offering all the provinces such powers, and have suggested an alternative that rejects decentralization, it is not likely we will be able to stop the Mulroney government from beginning to implement its decentralization agenda. One hopes they will be defeated before they complete it; but we need an interim strategy.

We must demand two things once the process is underway: national standards for all programs up for grabs; and the right of the people of each province to decide, by referendum, whether to opt out of national institutions. The demand for national standards will be part of the strategy to force provincial referenda because, if the federal government opts out of funding programs, it will be almost impossible for it to enforce standards. Only by referendum can provincial politicians be given the authority to opt out of Canada. A referendum vote *not* to opt out will ensure national standards.

Canadians can begin organizing for a "let the people decide" campaign immediately. Well before the next federal election this crisis is going to be upon us. We must be ready.

Step Five: Challenge the Parties
This step is the most directly political and absolutely critical. It requires mapping out our political strategy for the next federal election by preparing the ground work now.

The 1988 election posed a strategic dilemma for opponents of the government. There were two choices for an opposition vote, as the Liberals and the NDP had fairly similar positions on the issue of free trade. The results confirmed a Conservative victory, even though most Canadians opposed the government's platform.

At this point, it is unclear where the two major opposition parties will stand by the next election, as they are at different stages of developing trade and economic policy. Canadians are feeling deeply frustrated at the lack of a passionate or coherent opposition to the Mulroney agenda in Ottawa. Public rage at the government should be an opposition leader's dream; yet there seems to be no clear voice at the national level.

Here are our recommendations to prepare for the next federal election.

Reject the Reform

The sudden rise of the Reform Party should come as no surprise, given the leadership vacuum in Canada. Reformers offer a sympathetic ear and simple answers to Canadians feeling disenfranchised and cut off from political power. They promise a new Canada, equality of all the provinces and all people, deep cuts to public service "fat," and a return to the values of the past. Canadians are longing for straight talk and positive answers. They are feeling helpless in the face of gale-force winds of international economic change. Some are seeking solace and refuge in the Reform Party, and its philosophical siblings, the National Citizens' Coalition, the Confederation of Regions Party in Atlantic Canada, and the Alliance for the Preservation of English in Canada.

However, a serious look will reveal that Reformers are just Tories in a hurry. They subscribe to a U.S.–style free-market economy and would hasten continental free trade. They would redesign Canada's social, transportation, and economic policies to conform to the new continental agenda, exactly as the Tories are doing. The Reform Party manual describes the party aim as seeking to "maximize the benefits of our unique geographic and economic relationship with the United States." They would also entrench property rights in the Charter, a move that is opposed by women's groups, among others. (Property rights would then likely override provincial family law and workplace equality legislation.)

A Reform government would massively privatize remaining federal assets, implement full deregulation of the energy sector (so export deals would be made between transnational seller and transnational buyer without government interference), and kill marketing boards, supply management for agricultural products, and all subsidies and tariffs in the farm sector.

Universal social programs, including Medicare, would be turned over to the provinces, who would be permitted to dismantle them. The Reform Party opposes national child care; foreign aid; and grants to environmental, women's, and ethnic groups. It would cut off all funding to Canada's aboriginal people, letting them fend for themselves. Reformers will not negotiate any deal with Quebec that recognizes its special need for linguistic and cultural protection. They are prepared to let Quebec leave Confederation and have stated openly that they are prepared to be the party that oversees the dismantling of Canada. Reform booster Link Byfield, publisher of *Western Report*, says that the Reform's refusal to seek seats in Quebec makes it the only "honest broker" as "we watch Quebec puff and blow and make fools of us." Byfield awaits with glee someone who will put Quebec in its place.

Reformers are best known, however, for their opposition to the official policies of bilingualism and multiculturalism. Preston Manning insinuates that these policies favour francophones, immigrants, and visible minorities. Scapegoating falls on receptive ears in hard times of high unemployment. Maria Bohuslawsky, a reporter for the *Ottawa Citizen*, quotes Reg Gosse, who is spearheading the Reform's push into central Canada. Gosse discusses how to get "aborigines" off welfare, and how to eliminate government funding to the "ethnicals." He spoke about bringing to Canada a "better quality" of immigrant. Said one Reform supporter, "If a raghead or turbantop comes to this country, a government employee goes with them to a furniture store and a car lot and says 'You pick out what you want and we'll pay for it.' "

The politics of bigotry are the politics of fear. Canadians must reject them. Programs such as multiculturalism can always be improved; but Reformers are targetting myths, not facts. Canada's multiculturalism policy is aimed at integrating different ethnic groups into Canadian society by providing equality of opportunity and encouraging the rich cultural diversity that is one of the fundamental ways our country differs from the United States. Our commitment to bilingualism does not force anglophones to speak French. As D'Iberville Fortier, commissioner of Official Languages, explains, "The Official Languages Act was necessary in the name of history and fairness. Ottawa simply had to stop being a foreign government to the French-speakers of Canada."

The Reform Party is not the answer Canadians are seeking. Reformers represent their platform as populist and talk of "people power," but their policies would only destroy the national integrity of Canada, breaking the country into richer and poorer regions. It would hasten the growth of an emerging underclass of natives, visible minorities, and sole-support mothers that looks increasingly like the underclass of Washington, New York, and Miami.

Push the Liberals
Every Liberal member of Parliament was sent to Ottawa to oppose the Mulroney free-trade agenda. The party and its leader campaigned almost exclusively on this issue. Yet, all the signs point to a reversal of the party's position on free trade and its historic defence of strong national institutions. The constitutional resolution unanimously adopted by the Quebec wing of the federal Liberal party sounds like Tory policy. It accepts as its context the need for Canada to reorganize its economic structure to create a more "competitive" climate for Canadian business in the "new world economy."

The resolution calls for a "profoundly reformed federal system," a "new apportionment of powers," including "the determination of the level of government most capable of adequately responding to the needs of the population," and the elimination of the overlapping of federal and provincial jurisdictions (a code phrase for decentralization). The party of Jean Chrétien, who opposed the Meech Lake Accord as he believed it would have fragmented Canada, now embraces the right of all provinces to withdraw from national shared-cost programs with full financial compensation. It entirely accepts the notion of Canada Inc., a country that is little more than the sum of its bottom lines.

More disturbing, however, is an internal document being given wide credence in the party, written by its trade critic, Roy MacLaren. The paper analyses the options open to Canada with regard to the Canada-U.S. Free Trade Agreement and the process of extending free trade to the southern hemisphere. While acknowledging the "harmonizing" effect the deal has had on Canada's economy, MacLaren advises against getting out of it. He warns of dire financial consequences to Canada's economy. Taking a page from the speeches of Brian Mulroney and the BCNI's Thomas d'Aquino, he warns that abrogation of the free-trade deal would have serious consequences for Canadian unity. MacLaren sees real advantages in the deal: "As a result of the FTA Canada is no longer simply a market of twenty-six million, but is now a viable springboard to a market of some two hundred and fifty million." He even has some praise for the trilateral deal with Mexico.

His recommendation is to attempt to balance Canada's lack of equality in the North American situation by declaring Canada's economy "wide open" to the rest of the world, even if Canada has to do it unilaterally. Accepting that transnationals "offer more certainty in exploiting international markets," MacLaren advocates ensuring that Canada become "a secure and competitive destination for foreign investment."

To protect Canada from the obvious dangers of suddenly exposing all Canadian industry to wide-open international competition, the Liberal trade critic argues the need for a "far-reaching industrial policy." Traditionally, an industrial policy is a means whereby government and industry work together, building on a country's strengths to provide for its needs. Such collaboration requires government involvement in the running of the economy and in the redistribution of wealth. However, the most fundamental purpose of the Canada-U.S. Free Trade Agreement is to limit the role of government in North American transnational business. The Tory definition of an industrial policy is the transformation of government into a facilitator for the big corporations. Period.

A close reading of the Liberal trade document reveals that a Tory-type industrial policy is what is being considered by the Liberal party. The obvious next steps would be more privatization and deregulation, an end to government support of agriculture, and deeper cuts to public spending on education and health.

If the constitutional resolution and MacLaren's document are the underpinnings of the Liberal party's next election platform, Canadians concerned about the destruction of the country are not going to be able to support them.

Another concern about the Liberal party is its traditional indebtedness to the corporate sector through campaign contributions. This concern has never been more relevant than in the funding of the next election. This indebtedness will constrain the party from implementing the "Take Back the Nation" strategy recommended here. The Liberal party must make a clear choice: either allow the corporations to dictate party policy or break its dependence and refuse these donations.

Challenge the NDP

The federal NDP has taken a much clearer position on both the issues of continental free trade and the need for national institutions. Leader Audrey McLaughlin is on record that the party would abrogate the free-trade agreement if it formed the next government. Trade critic Dave Barrett has been a vociferous and passionate foe of trilateral free trade.

However, the NDP response to these and other contentious issues has been largely reactive rather than proactive. Canadians are hungry for political leaders to explain what is happening in clear, concise, and honest terms. The NDP has been too soft on the Reform Party; as the most obvious alternative to the Reform, it should be leading the assault against it. Provincial NDP leaders are not showing leadership regarding the issues of free trade and decentralization. Mike Harcourt of British Columbia, for example, spins a line on the merits of decentralization that is not much different from that of the federal Conservatives. They must be challenged to support the national goals of Canadians.

The NDP may be best suited to make the connections between the constitutional crisis and the Mulroney agenda of decentralization. However, it has stopped short of rallying the Canadian people to this analysis. It is afraid to talk about Quebec when it debates its constitutional position and remains, as a result, a minor player in the upcoming negotiations.

Finally, the NDP is not preparing Canadians to implement a "Take Back the Nation" strategy, including the abrogation of the free-trade agreement. It is not enough to make promises. Canadians must be made aware of concrete policies and their consequences.

Pre-Election Strategy

Canadians can become directly involved in the pre-election strategy now. They must publicly expose the Reform Party for the reactionary force that it is and work openly to defeat it.

Canadians can push the Liberal party to reject the MacLaren alternative and decentralization, and to develop a position on abrogation of the free-trade agreement. It must be encouraged to develop alternative policies to the right-wing corporate agenda. This will defeat the corporate forces within the party that have gained the upper hand.

Canadians who are members of the Liberal party or wish to be, must become active in riding associations and policy committees, urging the party to clarify its positions and restore the Liberal party to the best of its roots. They must also urge the leadership to put the needs of their country before the interests of their party.

Canadians can work to stiffen the NDP's spine in preparing the country for the fight ahead and developing forceful economic and political alternatives to the Mulroney agenda. Such action by the NDP could tilt the balance within the Liberal party and force it to adopt a "Take Back the Nation" strategy. Canadians who are members of the NDP or who wish to be, must become active now, lobbying the party to take a more proactive, educational role and to put the needs of their country before the interests of their party.

As the position of the Liberal party becomes more clearly defined, it will be easier to advance a strategy for the defeat of the Tories. If only one opposition party is actively articulating a solid criticism of the corporate agenda and viable alternatives to it, the citizens' movement, including the Council of Canadians and Action Canada Network, will likely openly support that party.

If both opposition parties adopt a "Take Back the Nation" platform, we believe Canadians will have to develop a plan for a "strategic vote." This might entail asking Canadians to support a particular candidate in selected ridings rather than blanket support of one or another party. In perhaps twenty ridings where the NDP is not likely to win, people would be asked to support the Liberals as the best way to defeat the Tories. In twenty ridings where the Liberals are not likely to win, people would be asked to support the NDP candidate.

Canadians could also organize to back nomination candidates for the two opposition parties who will fight the Mulroney free-trade agenda. We need to send to Parliament candidates whose commitment to a "Take Back the Nation" platform is on record.

Finally, the next Parliament is likely to be a five-way split, with no party a clear winner. In this event, the Mulroney Conservatives, the Bloc Québécois, and the Reform Party are likely to form an alliance, however temporary, to implement their common goals. It will be necessary for the Liberals and the NDP to form a coalition to oppose this development. It is for this reason that it is urgent that the nationalist forces within the Liberal party take the ascendency. It must be our goal to ensure that in a coalition situation, this arm of the party will override the corporate arm and join forces with the NDP to defeat the Mulroney-supported transnational agenda.

It is common these days for Canadians to decry the lack of leadership in our country. This is only partially true. Brian Mulroney knows exactly where he is going. He must not be allowed to take us with him.

Looking for one person to rescue us is, in the long run, an abdication of our obligations. Each and every one of us must make a personal commitment to take permanent responsibility for the future of our country. When we ask the question, "Who will save Canada?" the only answer can be found in the mirror. We must all take a long look.

Says Newfoundland activist Dorothy Inglis, "Our combined numbers must be used to fight tooth and nail to re-establish the institutions that once bound this country together. We must be the patriots with the new vision based on the old commitment." Adds Jon K. Grant, president of Quaker Oats, "Are we Canadians prepared to walk down this difficult road of 'short-term pain for long-term gain' and secure Canada for future generations? If so, all of us can do our part and encourage honest and thoughtful Canadians to take on the mantle of political leadership. It is indeed a high calling that generations to come will thank us for."

Bishop Remi DeRoo writes, "We have reached a time of reckoning, a moment of truth. If Canada is to maintain its identity, all those who care about our common future need to get involved. Authentic hope can read the data of despair, see through it, and rediscover the bedrock values that energize people for renewed conquests. Believe there is nothing beyond the power of determined people who truly love Canada and are dedicated to the survival of our country as a creative force in the global community of nations."

No matter who wins the next election, Canadians must never again become complacent and trusting of "someone else" to look after our democracy. The coalitions we have built must stay together and grow. We must establish the tools of democracy, the citizens' instruments to ensure we have access to the decision makers and they respond to us. The new world agenda will not depart with Mulroney or his party. The fight will be with us for many years.

ORGANIZATIONS

For further information, contact:

The Council of Canadians
A non-profit, non-partisan national organization devoted to the enhancement and preservation of Canadian
sovereignty.

1006 — 251 Laurier Avenue West
Ottawa, Ontario
Canada K1P 5J6

Telephone: (613) 233-2773

Action Canada Network
A coalition of forty major organizations formed to fight
the free-trade agreement and the corporate agenda.

904 — 251 Laurier Avenue West
Ottawa, Ontario
Canada K1P 5J6

Telephone: (613) 233-1764

INDEX